THE TOOLBOX
For life's little emergencies

Judith te Huia

Published in 2016 by Te Ana

Copyright © Judith Te Huia 2016

ISBN Paperback: 978-0-9945565-0-9
Ebook: 978-0-9945565-1-6

All rights reserved. No part of this publication may be reproduced, stored in a retrieval system, or transmitted in any form or by any means, electronic, mechanical, photocopying, recording or otherwise, without the prior permission of the copyright owner.

National Library of Australia
Cataloguing-in-Publication Entry

Illustrations by Lynda Freeman

Published with the help of Indie Authors World

To Hully, Audrey and Barb. Without their support and encouragement, this would still be a thought.

Acknowledgements

There are a few people I need to thank for making this book become a reality. To Christine McPherson for making the editing process so easy. To Lynda Freeman for the beautiful illustrations in the book and to Kim and Sinclair Macleod who made this whole process an absolute pleasure. I found in Kim a kindred spirit she made time to listen and give suggestions that were very much appreciated. A very different experience from my first publishing adventure and last but not least to Hully my husband whom at times thought I was attached to my computer and would cart me off down the street to have a break thank you.

My letter to Robin

I know you are at the point of thinking you can't do this any more. The struggle is just becoming too much. You have tried the traditional medical model but don't really want to go down that path again, so you are asking yourself, "What else is out there?" "Where can I go to find it?" I know you would like to try meditation, but you told me it all sounds too complicated. It doesn't have to be. I can teach you how to do it.

You want to have some control back in your life, to have some peace, less stress, to stop worrying about day-to-day stuff. You want to find some time for yourself, some happiness, but you don't think it is possible.

This is where I can help you and offer you the tools to get you to that place you want to go.

It's not about trying to control situations around you. It is about how you react to them.

This book is an introduction to the tools you can learn to use to help you react differently, to connect with the problems and gain different solutions. It is about taking you on a journey of self-care to find your own inner help, wisdom and peace through meditation, relaxation techniques, changing your thoughts, using visualisation, taking care of self, and not feeling guilty.

We will walk through this book together, and when you reach the end you will be a very different person than when you began.

Remember, this is just the beginning of living your life in a more positive, fulfilling way.

Love and light,

Judith

Introduction

If you are reading this, it means you are looking to make some changes in your life. You may have already begun. You might be frustrated, craving "me" time, anxious, feeling disconnected, or that no-one is listening to you. You feel you can't go on any more, you are just exhausted. Perhaps you are juggling too many aspects in your life and you no longer know who you are. I know this can be hard – everyone wants to avoid discomfort – but it is important that you don't censor your understanding.

Perhaps you have already tried to get help, been to see a holistic practitioner, visited your GP, or talked to friends. I know you are committed to resolving this situation and I really empathize with your frustration that these other solutions haven't completely worked out.

You are feeling alone with your thoughts, or you're consulting people who aren't experts. With this, there is no partnership. As supportive as some others may be, they don't know the right questions to ask to help move you forward. They have probably not walked in your shoes.

In order for you to be empowered, feel less stressed, more in control at work and home, you need to have solutions that are tailored to suit your needs and lifestyle. You need something that is unique. To have someone who is with you every step of the way. If the previous solutions have been overly intellectual, then what is needed is for transformational work that involves physicality.

My passion for helping people to bring about positive change and empowerment in their lives comes from a time when I worked in a very stressful workplace environment and found myself the target of bullying and harassment. I was tired all the time, not sleeping, unproductive, and certainly had no clarity or peace of mind. Learning meditation, relaxation techniques, and positive psychology, was a lifesaver for me, and I could not imagine my life without them now.

This is what I hope to give you in this book – the steps to get you to that place you want to go. I will teach you:

- to meet challenges by learning the skills to balance personal, family, and work.
- to identify the symptoms of anxiety, stress, depression, and grief.
- how to live your life in balance and take responsibility for your own life choices.
- how to meditate.
- to understand self-esteem and self-awareness.
- how to take a ground approach to self-care.
- how to create and bring about change.
- where we hold and feel change in our bodies, and how to deal with it.
- how to create a gratitude journal.
- some of the best and most effective focusing techniques.

Bringing about change in our lives takes time, but it can happen if we want it to. It is up to us. We can't blame others for our lives not turning out the way we want them to; we have to have the courage to make the changes.

THE TOOLBOX

There cannot be a stressful crisis next week. My schedule is already full.

Henry Kissinger

◇◇◇◇◇◇◇◇◇◇◇◇◇◇◇◇◇◇◇◇◇◇◇◇◇◇◇◇◇◇

The ability to transform:

"The greatest weapon against stress is our ability to choose one thought over the other."

William James

Chapter 1 - Our Wellbeing

"If you are depressed you are living in the past.
If you are anxious you are living in the future.
If you are at peace you are living in the present."
Lao Tzu

Our lives are full of stress: transitions, growing responsibilities, our goals, and our work. We may encounter more stressful situations at different times and in various stages as we traverse through our life's journey; even coping with happy situations can sometimes be stressful.

If we are not careful, stress can consume us. It can create issues in different areas of our life, including:

- Difficulties achieving a work/life balance, due to being overtired.
- Creating an inefficient working environment by having a poorly balanced day.
- Health concerns, including depression, anxiety, insomnia and listlessness, and more.
- Diminished quality of life.
- Developing low self-esteem, self-doubt, or a feeling of unworthiness.
- Substance abuse.
- Feeling disconnected from yourself, as if you are losing your identity.

- ❋ Frequent feelings of frustration.
- ❋ Inability to carve out "Me-Time".
- ❋ Feeling unheard.
- ❋ Constant feelings of being overwhelmed.

Learning how to relieve stress can actually improve your wellbeing, create work/life balance, increase your chances of success, make you a healthier and more efficient person, and – most importantly – increase the overall quality of your life.

You might have already taken one or more of these steps in seeking help to manage issues that are causing you stress:

- ❋ Talked to your doctor.
- ❋ Visited a counsellor.
- ❋ Visited websites.
- ❋ Talked to your friends.
- ❋ Taken medication.
- ❋ Tried stress relief techniques.

With the above, there is no partnership. As supportive as some others may be, they don't know the right questions to ask you to help you move forward.

In order for you to empower yourself, feel less stressed, and to be more in control at work and home, you need to have solutions which are tailored to suit *your* needs and *your* lifestyle. Even if you have already changed some aspects of your lifestyle, you will still greatly benefit from something that is unique; to have someone who is with you every step of the way.

This is what I hope to give you – a set of tools to put in a toolbox that you keep adding to. Tools to assist you as you traverse though your life, to empower yourself and to get you to the place where you truly want to be. Enough of them that they can make your life smoother, even through all of life's twists and turns.

The Toolbox

The tools in this book will help empower you, and will at times challenge your thinking. They include:

- Skills to balance personal life, family life, and work.
- The means to identify the symptoms of anxiety, stress, depression, and grief.
- Learning how to live your life in balance and take responsibility.
- Lessons on how to live in the present moment by challenging you to step out of your comfort zone.

Most importantly, I will teach you to use one of the most powerful tools we have in our modern world: meditation.

My promise to you is that I will walk beside you all the way as you navigate through this journey, to help you and guide you to make a positive difference in your life and the lives of others. *Life is a journey and it can't be hurried.* It demands patience, emotional energy, and courage. You do not have to do it alone. I will help you.

Living in the Present

Learning to live in the present moment and not dwelling on the past or the future is something to aim for. Focusing on how much better it was in the past, or to look to the future as your saving grace, wastes a lot of energy. By all means, have your dreams – they are really important, so hang onto them – but you need to be living in the present moment. Be here, be now, and be in this moment. I am certainly not saying don't have dreams or goals; I am saying be ready to revise them if necessary.

When you are living the life you are meant to be living, change and flexibility is a part of flowing harmoniously with life. Gita Bellin said, "The only way to deal with the future is to function efficiently in the now." Keep it uncomplicated and try not to get caught up in the dramas that are going on around you on a personal level.

Checklist

1 - Understanding the symptoms of stress, depression and grief, can help us to understand if we may be suffering from any one of them.

2 - We realise that there is help out there and we must not be afraid to ask for it.

3 - Taking care of ourselves is necessary and we must not feel guilty about it.

Chapter 2 - Meeting Challenge

"There are days I drop words of comfort on myself like falling leaves and remember that it is enough to be taken care of by myself."

Brian Andreas

Balancing Personal Family and Work

Are you in a position where another person's wellbeing depends upon you? This might be your children, your spouse, your work, or even just caring for your family.

To be able to give adequate care to anyone in your sphere of influence, you must know how to take care of yourself first. If you are a mother/father with small children, or have a child with disabilities, or even if it's just yourself and your partner, ask yourself these questions:

* How much time do I get for myself?
* Am I aware of how I am really feeling at this moment?
* Have my feelings and emotions been pushed into the background?
* Do I put everyone's needs first before my own?

Contemplate these points for a moment. Don't rush into doing them all at once. When you feel ready, try the next set of questions and answer them as honestly as you can.

Do you also work in any kind of professional capacity?
Yes/No

Are you drawn away from home and those you care for in order to earn a wage?
Yes/No

Do you make time for yourself?
Yes/No

Do you spend time on your own?
Yes/No

Do you find it difficult being in your own company?
Yes/No

What do you do in the time that is yours?

```
[                                                          ]
```

Do you ask for help when you need it?
Yes/No

Do you feel guilty that you are having time for yourself?
Yes/No

Do you have a support network?
Yes/No

If yes, who is your support network?

```
[                                                          ]
```

How would you describe your coping skills?

```
[                                                          ]
```

These are really important questions to ask yourself, because as a caregiver and provider of nourishment for yourself or others (whether it's financial, emotional or spiritual), it's all too easy to lose your identity.

When this happens, when your own sense of self becomes unclear and your day solely revolves around others, it is too easy for symptoms of anxiety, self-doubt, or unworthiness to start to show.

Being overtired, not eating properly, having a poorly balanced day, ignoring or overriding your feelings, can lead to the slippery slope of anxiety or depression.

So what are you going to do about it?

How can you change your life so that you can still care for others while looking after yourself?

How can you find time to work on your self-development?

You may make up excuses as to why you don't have time, but can you really afford not to?

Knowing the Symptoms

"And knowing is half the battle."
G.I Joe

Knowing the symptoms of anxiety, stress, depression, and grief, while also knowing there is help available to you, is a step towards coping with and managing these conditions. Understanding your own mental, emotional, and spiritual processes when under stress or in crisis-mode, is also really important.

In the healing process, acknowledging the individual, knowing that you need to work through each symptom thoroughly in order to bring about a healthy outcome, will have you well on the way to enjoying a balanced and positive outlook on life. These are vital tools which, once learned and understood, can be added to your toolbox of coping skills.

Some Symptoms of Anxiety

Often symptoms of anxiety are felt in the body, and people will go to a doctor thinking there is something physically wrong. I'm sure you've felt mild symptoms of anxiety at times in your life, but when they stop being moderate you have a problem that needs attention. Your body has a primal reaction to dangerous and overwhelming situations and is more commonly understood as the "flight or fight" response.

In the past, ancient man would have been running from dinosaurs or other dangerous predators. It still feels like that to this day when we deal with modern living, even if your dangerous predator comes in the form of the power bill, your boss, or even waving your children goodbye as they go to school.

Some of the symptoms of anxiety, or "flight or fight", are:

* Heart palpitations
* Trembling or shaking
* Feeling sick or nauseous
* Cold or clammy hands
* Hot flushes or chills
* Increased heart rate
* Dry mouth
* Trouble sleeping
* Difficulty focusing

These symptoms can be controlled with relaxation techniques and by acknowledging your own feelings and emotions. Doing this will put you in touch with your body, which often has the best answers to positive self-healing.

Additionally, positive self-talk, affirmations, gentle exercise, personal development, sleep, and reduced alcohol and caffeine consumption, will all enhance your ability to handle anxiety. I would hasten to add that should your feelings of anxiety persist beyond the management tools listed previously, you should seek additional professional help.

So before we go any further let us look at what we can do to help you right now.

I am going to show you how to do a very easy relaxation technique, so let's begin. I'll start by getting you to focus on your breathing. You can do this at any time, as long as you can do it safely.

- Closing your eyes, just take in a big deep breath, hold it for the count of three and then breathe out slowly. Repeat this exercise six times and then see how you feel when you have finished. It brings everything into balance, doesn't it? It stops you feeling panicky and allows you to feel calmer. You can do this any time you start to feel yourself becoming tense or anxious.

- Another little tool is positive self-talk. Once again, if you feel yourself becoming anxious, just start saying to yourself, "I am okay, it is okay. Just keep saying it until you feel yourself becoming calmer.

- Changing negative thoughts to positive can really change how you view life. Try it, it works.

Some Symptoms of Stress

We have all experienced stress, and no doubt you have a pretty good idea what generates it in your life and the havoc it can wreak. Most of us would like to have less stress, but it can be difficult to eliminate it entirely because most of us work, have families, and if you're not already in a personal relationship, then perhaps you're looking to start one.

Sometimes we need stress to motivate us and generate alertness and so on, but when it is prolonged or severe, it can dangerously increase health issues – mental health problems in particular – so striking a balance of activity and relaxation is a must.

Stress symptoms can include:

- Reflux
- Irritable bowel
- Ulcers
- Indigestion
- Diarrhoea, constipation
- Heart disease

- Asthma
- Immune system-related disease
- Cancer
- Muscle spasms
- Depression
- Anxiety
- Alcohol and drug misuse and dependence

What induces stress differs from person to person, as do the symptoms, but it can affect us profoundly. Stress is not just something in your mind; it can trigger a whole series of biochemical changes in your body that are experienced physically as well as psychologically.

Stress can be major, or it can appear minor, and usually occurs as we struggle with life-changing events and ongoing challenges. But, like anxiety, the good news is that stress can be managed and kept to a healthy level. Have a look at the techniques used to manage anxiety again, as the same techniques can be used to help reduce stress. I cannot emphasise enough the importance of getting professional help when you feel you can't cope any more. You are not a failure in any way; in fact, the complete opposite is true. The ability to ask for help shows an unbelievable amount of strength.

Some tools to help with stress

- Make time for yourself each day.
- Don't feel guilty about it. A healthy you is a healthy family. Even if this is just having a bath or going for a walk.
- Keep a journal – just write how you have been feeling; it can help.
- Have a good cry; it is part of the healing process.
- Find someone to talk to.
- Take life one day at a time.

- Practice your breathing techniques.
- Find a good listener or a counsellor.
- Take care of yourself.
- Get regular exercise with gardening, walking, yoga, or Tai Chi.
- Practice Relaxation Meditation, which is in the chapter on meditation.
- Keep up with your hobbies, passions, and anything you love doing.
- Never be afraid or ashamed to ask for help; you are human, not superhuman.

What is the difference between depression and "the blues"?

Over one million people in Australia live with depression. Over two million have anxiety disorder. How do you know if you have "the blues", or are suffering from depression?

The blues

Everyone will experience the blues at some point in their lives. The feeling of sadness, grief, loneliness or lack of motivation when going through a difficult life experience, is part of being human. They can often be helpful in a sense; life's way of letting you know that something is amiss, which is your cue to make changes in your life. Most of the time, you can continue to function and you know that you will bounce back – and you do.

What is depression?

Depression is a serious condition. While we have all felt sad and low in mood, from time to time you may experience these feelings very deeply and profoundly, often without a reason. Have you ever found it difficult to function on a day-to-day basis? Have normal activities become increasingly more difficult to cope with?

Have you ever had trouble getting out of bed? This is more than just laziness; it's a profound desire to have no interaction at all with the outside world. Activities that you once enjoyed are harder to take part in? Depression becomes a serious problem when these feelings persist.

How do you know if someone has depression?

If a person has been feeling sad, down, or unhappy most of the time **for more than two weeks,** or has lost interest in most of their activities.

Depression symptoms can include:

- Not wanting to go out any more.
- Withdrawing from close family and friends.
- Finding it difficult to concentrate.
- Feeling overwhelmed, irritable, unhappy, sad, tired all the time.
- Having negative thoughts, i.e. "I'm a failure." "I'm worthless." "Life's not worth living."
- Feeling sick and run-down, not sleeping.
- Experiencing headaches and muscle pains, significant weight loss or gain.

Some factors which may contribute to depression are:

- A family history of depression.
- Hormonal changes.
- Loss of a loved one.
- Medication.
- Medical conditions.
- Abuse.
- Personality type.

Left untreated, depression can last for weeks, months or years. Early attention is important. It is a serious disorder. However, when treated properly, you can hope to expect a full recovery. In some cases, anti-depressant medication will be required in combination with personal development and the techniques that have been mentioned for anxiety and stress.

Depression is not something to take lightly, and can sometimes require immediate professional attention. As mentioned previously, it is important that you acknowledge all parts of yourself in order to heal. Use your self-care management techniques and, if your feelings are still troubling you, seek further help from your Doctor or another health professional about getting appropriate treatment.

You can find a Depression Checklist on Beyond Blue's website. http://www.beyondblue.org.au

Understanding the difference between feeling "blue" and being depressed can make a difference in the quality of life for an affected individual. With proper treatment, depression can be managed, and individuals can live more enjoyable and productive lives.

Some Symptoms of Grief

Grief is the reaction we have to losses of significance in our lives. This can include:

- Loss of a pet.
- Loss of a job or employment.
- Loss of health.
- Loss of a loved one.
- Ending a relationship.
- Loss of plans, goals, or a dream.

One of the biggest losses that we will experience is the death of a loved one. Bereavement grief is difficult to cope with, and we all experience it differently. It often shows up as a physical and psychological reaction to the changes which have been forced upon us in a significant and meaningful way.

Grief symptoms can include:

- Sadness, anger
- Breathlessness, physical weakness
- Confusion, crying, withdrawing from family and friends

How we experience grief, and for how long, depends upon many factors, such as how much the person meant to us, the role we played in caring for them, and how strongly we identified with their experiences.

What was our state of mind like at the time? The state of our emotional, spiritual and physical wellness is also important. What other factors were happening in our lives at the time of their passing? It is not only a major loss in itself, but it can often mean other losses as well, such as:

- Loss of income or financial security.
- Loss of routine, stability.
- Loss of future together.
- Loss of mutual friends.
- Loss of opportunities.

Grief does diminish with time. Sometimes the pain of grief can increase in the first few months after a death, as not only the reality of what has happened is sinking in, but the support structures which were initially in place start to fall away.

But grief is a journey, and it cannot be hurried. It demands patience, emotional energy, and courage. You are starting a new phase in your life and adapting to new challenges, but you must also find the reserves of strength to call upon hope, courage, and faith. We experience many things when grieving – both emotional and mental – and we can be experiencing them all at the same time. Shock, pain, sadness, anger, guilt, anxiety, mental disorganisation, and feeling overwhelmed, relief, and loneliness. These are all normal reactions when you are grieving.

Sometimes it may seem easier to avoid grief, as nobody really wants to have it in his or her life, but it is a healthy part of living. When we try to avoid grief, it doesn't go away; it just becomes more overwhelming. The harder we try, the worse it becomes.

The Toolbox

A healthy way to grieve is having the ability to move between the challenges of what you may need to deal with – the pain and emotion, and the practical aspect of day-to-day living. It may at first seem impossible, but when you look at yourself and what you are feeling, and analyse your reactions, sometimes a path of action and reaction becomes clear.

<u>Some key tools to help with grief:</u>

- Take time for yourself each day.
- Keep a journal – it can help.
- Have a good cry; it is part of the healing process.
- Avoid making any major decisions for at least a year.
- Take life one day at a time.
- Writing a letter to the one you have lost can really help.
- Get help with financial matters.
- Find a good listener or grief counsellor.
- Take care of yourself.
- Get regular exercise with gardening, walking, yoga, or Tai Chi.
- Relaxation Meditation.
- Keep up with your hobbies, passions, and anything you love doing.
- Being mindful.

I found when dealing with grief that the saying "time heals" is true. As time passes, you do manage better.

<u>Helpful Tips</u>

- Meditating for 10 minutes in the morning helps you to be prepared for the day by creating an internal energetic balance. I have created the heart meditation, which is a beautiful gentle meditation. (Meditation is in the next chapter.)
- Seek help from a friend or professional.

- ✹ Use affirmations.
- ✹ A good point to remember is, "Am I going to allow this to make me unhappy for the rest of the day or just for this period of time?"
- ✹ Write in your journal.

Making sure that you have "me time" is vitally important for your own mental, emotional, spiritual, and physical wellness. Your family and loved ones will benefit from you being well and happy. We can often be so caught up in making sure everyone else is looked after that we forget about the most important person: You. How can you care for someone else when your own happiness is not being taken care of? Here are a few quick suggestions for enhancing your mental and emotional wellness by doing everyday, ordinary things.

Self-care management techniques:

- ✹ Walk.
- ✹ Use relaxation techniques.
- ✹ Lessen the amount of caffeine taken daily.
- ✹ Eat a healthy diet: three main meals a day – don't just graze.
- ✹ Be kind to yourself.
- ✹ Do something just for you.
- ✹ Have your hair cut.
- ✹ Soak in the bath.
- ✹ Sit in the sun.
- ✹ Do nothing.
- ✹ Do yoga or Tai Chi.
- ✹ Ask a friend to look after your children.
- ✹ Never be afraid or ashamed to ask for help; you are human, not superhuman.
- ✹ Talk to someone about how you are feeling, don't bottle it up.

The Toolbox

- Walking, jogging, and running really help with mental wellness, even if it's only a few laps around the garden.
- Meeting up with friends is vital.
- Keep up your interests to whatever extent you can.

Often the symptoms of anxiety, stress, depression and grief are due to us living our lives out of balance and needing to take responsibility for our own choices in life. But it can all be changed. There is always hope, if you are willing to make a positive difference in your life.

Like grief, life is a journey and it cannot be hurried. It demands patience, emotional energy, and courage.

Checklist

1 - Sometimes the symptoms of anxiety, stress, and depression can mean that some part of our life may be out of balance.

2 - Walking, meditating and talking to someone can really help.

3 - Keeping a positive outlook can change how we think.

Chapter 3- Meditation for Wellness

"The Way to do is to be."

Lao Tzu

Benefits of Meditation

Research carried out at the Mayo Clinic in the US concluded that meditation could give you a sense of calm, peace, and balance which benefits both your emotional wellbeing and your overall health.

Meditation is one of the most powerful tools we have in our modern world, and its benefits are many; it is a natural relaxation and healing process which focuses on calming the mind and relaxing the physical body. Many cultures have preserved some practice of this ritualistic technique, whether in the form of prayer, reflection, or moving meditation such as Tai Chi or Yoga. These practices promote changes from the normal levels of perception that may result in the feeling of union and greater wellbeing.

There has been a lot of research to find out how much of an impact meditation has in our everyday lives and health matters. It's been found to hold a wide range of helpful and healing benefits across a broad spectrum, and is now included in medical mainstream practice which promotes it as a great way to avoid general stress. In some cases it has helped people to reduce their medications, in addition to relieving and aiding in pain management.

Look at the stress we put ourselves under with our need to achieve great success in our profession, and our need to maintain our lifestyle.

It does not allow much time, if any, for the pursuit of the spiritual self. But more and more people are now searching for balance and meaning in their lives, with some opting to remove themselves totally from the mainstream to live a life of peace, harmony, and self-sufficiency. If we don't want to go to this extreme, then making time to understand the benefits of spiritual development and incorporating meditation, spiritual and mindfulness practise into our lives is well worth the effort.

Meditation can help relieve:

* Stress-related disorders
* Blood pressure problems
* Circulatory disorders
* Headaches and migraines
* Muscular aches and pains
* Asthma and breathing difficulties
* Anxiety

These are just a few of the symptoms that can be relieved through meditation, but it takes time, practice, and patience to truly experience the full benefits.

When you first begin meditating, it's possible that your mind will still want to be in control. It certainly doesn't want to allow something else to take over and have it quieten down. This can be the most difficult part of meditation. To have the noisy mind go quiet and stop thinking is certainly a challenge. It will find a way to try and disrupt your calm as it honestly doesn't know how to stop and be quiet. Initially, there will be some chatter, but with time and patience, this will gradually stop.

The mind's job is to think, just as your eyes see and your ears hear. This is where meditation will help. It will assist the mind to rest and have a break rather than continually be busy from morning till night.

There are various types and forms of meditation, all of which are designed to appeal to different parts of your brain. Explore your options and try them all to see which method works best for you.

If you have a medical condition or other health problems, it's worth talking to your health care provider about whether you would benefit from learning to meditate.

Visualisation

This is a guided visual experience led by a meditation teacher or spiritual development teacher, and involves using the imagination to take the mind to a new "environment", such as swimming peacefully with dolphins or walking in a beautiful garden. It is a good place to start when you're initially trying to quieten your mind. Twenty minutes of this form of meditation will help you to feel centred and more relaxed.

If you don't have a meditation or spiritual development teacher, you can find CDs or downloads to guide you through meditation visualisation. I have a number of guided visual meditations available on my website.

Transcendental

Transcendental meditation is based on the concept of using mantras of short words or phrases, repeated continually in the mind. Mantras are selected on the basis of your temperament, occupation, and level of development. The mantra is usually chosen by a spiritual teacher to suit the individual student, and the student never discloses their mantra to another.

This form of meditation is practiced twice daily for fifteen to twenty minutes. It helps to settle the mind and is one of the most researched forms of meditation. You would need to go to a class to learn this form of meditation and to develop the discipline to hold your mind steady whilst you employ it.

Relaxation

Relaxation meditation is based on focusing attention on consecutive areas of the body and relaxing the muscles by tensing and releasing until the process is completed throughout the whole body. It allows the mind to be eased of the physical state of consciousness, and the student to enjoy a heightened sense of relaxation and wellbeing. This form of meditation is of benefit to those who may struggle with guided meditation. It is a gentle way of starting to learn about relaxing the body and mind. This form of meditation is used in hospitals, aged care facilities, counselling practices, and many other places. It can also be purchased on CDs and downloaded from the Internet.

Moving Meditation

You may like to try some form of moving meditation, such as Yoga or Tai Chi. In moving meditation you learn breathing techniques, the importance of posture, all about your musculature, movement, flow, balance, and of being centred. The art of visualisation and imagery is also practised in some cases.

Moving meditation is done slowly, exercising mindfulness of what you are doing at all times, and taking in what is around you rather than rushing through it or past it. You will become very aware of your body and muscle movements and your environment in ways that you hadn't previously. You'll also discover a new sense of grace and elegance within yourself.

Mindfulness Meditation

Mindfulness meditation is becoming very popular. It is a form of meditation that helps us stay in the moment and allows us to be present in the here and now, not focusing on the future or in the past. Mindfulness meditation is about the mind being calm and in harmony with the body. In other forms of meditation you tend to achieve an altered state of consciousness. In mindfulness meditation it is more about being aware of your thoughts, feelings and emotions, but not judging them.

Research suggests that mindfulness meditation may improve mood, decrease stress, and boost immune function. It is not necessary to close your eyes when practising mindfulness meditation, but if you feel more comfortable with them closed then do so.

This form of meditation can be done anywhere, such as at work or on the train. Perhaps, when you next feel that your stress levels are rising, just breathe normally, be aware of the thoughts you are having, and then take your thoughts back to your breathing. Doing this for a few moments can have beneficial results. The difference between mindfulness meditation and other forms of meditation is that you are still in an alert state, rather than going into a deeper meditative state. The Buddhist approach is that the mind and body are connected. Mindfulness meditation is better practised sitting up to allow the energy to flow freely.

Learning to meditate

There are many ways to meditate, but guided relaxation meditation is what we will be concentrating on in this book. You may not find it easy to visualise; some people feel more strongly, sense, hear, or just know things rather than see things. These senses are what we use when working with our perception. All you need do is focus, give yourself some time, and be patient with yourself.

It may take a while to work out which is the best meditation for you, as there are many different places to get CDs and DVDs. You can also try online but, as ever, the key is to feel comfortable and keep searching until you either find a teacher that you feel happy with, or a meditation that you like and which works well for you.

In any form of meditation or exercise, we need to set our intention. When I am going into meditation, my intention is that whatever I receive be in accordance with my highest good.

The Toolbox

Some do's and don'ts when meditating:

- Find a comfortable place to sit or lie.
- It is best to meditate early in the morning or at night. If this is not possible, during the day is fine, but try and meditate at the same time every day.
- Wear comfortable clothing, nothing restrictive.
- If sitting, place your hands comfortably on your lap or on the sides of your chair.
- Uncross your legs and hands.
- If lying on the floor, cover yourself with a blanket, as you may get cold while meditating (be aware it is possible to fall asleep while being in this position).
- Leave your logical mind in another room.

Creating Sacred Space

It is important when doing any kind of meditation that you create a space to work in and to have clear intent. There are many ways in which to do this: by using crystals; the Native American medicine wheel; asking Spirit; and for the Golden Rose Protection (higher form of white light) to surround you, and so on. It creates a safe space in which you can meditate.

Setting your sacred space

I want us to set up our psychical spiritual and mental space. It needs to be a quiet, relaxing area, where you can sit or lie comfortably. It needs to be telephone-free so that there are no interruptions.

Closing your eyes, quietly take a few deep breaths, and then ask that a sacred space be created for you to work in. Ask that the Golden Rose Protection be placed around you. Set your intention, which is what you hope to achieve from this exercise, and ask that you only work *with the Best of the Best and the Highest of the High.*

Relaxation meditation exercise

Let's try our first relaxation meditation; you can download this from my webpage.

Let your brain have its way for a minute. This is often easier said than done, as your brain suddenly realises someone is trying to control it. It takes a bit of practice but keep at it, as it is so beneficial. If it helps, you can find an object to focus on – such as a candle – then begin to bring your thoughts to the task at hand, and concentrate on your breathing. Remember to breathe in and breathe out until you feel you are ready to move into your meditation.

Another way of keeping focused is to find a mental object to train your attention on – a tree in your meditation forest; a flower in your mediation garden; or you can imagine a candle. Whatever works for you.

Relaxation meditation

- Close your eyes and ask for protection: Protection is creating a sacred space around your body as you allow yourself to do your meditation.
- Breathe in and out slowly for a few breaths.
- On the next in-breath, breathe deeply from the bottom of your diaphragm.
- Hold to the count of three.
- Release it slowly.
- Repeat this up to six times.
- Breathe in through your mouth and out through your nose.
- Start by relaxing the body.
- Begin at the toes.
- Screw up your toes as tightly as you can.
- Then release them slowly.
- Repeat this exercise three times.

- Move up to your calf muscles.
- Tighten them as tightly as you can.
- Then release slowly.
- Repeat this three times.
- Move up to your buttocks.
- Squeeze as hard as you can.
- Hold and release slowly.
- Repeat this three times.
- Tighten your hands into fists and clench them tightly.
- Release slowly.
- Repeat three times.
- Take your shoulders up to your ears.
- Hold them there to the count of ten.
- Then let them drop slowly.
- Repeat three times.
- Screw up your face tightly.
- Then smile.
- Repeat three times.
- When you are ready to finish, imagine your body is surrounded in a rainbow of colours.

Allow yourself to sit quietly for a moment and then, bringing your awareness back, become aware of your chair – or the floor, if you are lying on it – and wiggle your toes and hands, then slowly open your eyes and sit quietly for a few moments to allow yourself to become present in your mind and body.

You will find that your body will feel a lot more relaxed. The more slowly you do this exercise, the more benefit you will gain from it.

Using colour in meditation

Bringing colour into meditation is also a good way to do some healing on our bodies. When you are doing your breath work and you get the feeling that you need to bring in a colour, just imagine breathing it into your body on the in-breath. Even sending the colour straight to the part of your body that may need some healing, and imagining it surrounded and covered by the colour, really helps. The colour blue and green are used most in healing work.

Colour meditation

This next meditation is the colour meditation. It is just a short one and a good one to carry on straight after the relaxation meditation. If you want to do it on its own, prepare yourself as you have done for the relaxation meditation.

* Now breathe a colour into your body; start with any colour you choose.
* You will notice that each colour makes your body feel different.
* Imagine that you are breathing the colour in through the top of your head.
* Breathe it down your spine.
* Imagine on the in-breath that you are breathing in the colour you chose.
* This will help to relax your body.
* On the out-breath, you are releasing all the tension that your body is holding onto.
* Each time you get to the base of your spine, send the colour down both of your legs.
* Imagine it is flowing out of the soles of your feet, going into the earth, connecting you with Mother Earth.

- Allow your body to feel relaxed and connected to Mother Earth.
- Then imagine it flowing back up through the soles of your feet, up through your spine to the top of your head.
- You will start to feel yourself become lighter and more relaxed.
- If there are parts of your body that are tense, like across your shoulders, imagine sending a beautiful green blue colour into the muscles. Breathing the colour in and out, imagine you are releasing the tension.
- You can do this for any part of your body.
- When you are ready to finish, imagine your body is surrounded in a rainbow of colours.
- Allow yourself to sit quietly for a moment and then, bringing your awareness back, become aware of your chair – or the floor, if you are lying on it – and wiggle your toes and hands, then slowly open your eyes and sit quietly for a few moments to allow yourself to become present in your mind and body. When we are doing any form of relaxation or meditation we go into an altered state of awareness, so sitting for a moment allows us to come back into our conscious, waking state.

Heart healing meditation

Prepare yourself just as you have for the relaxation meditation.

- Close your eyes and allow your body to relax.
- Breathe in and breathe out slowly, concentrating on your breath.
- Repeat this for the next six breaths.
- On the next in-breath imagine you are sitting in the middle of a beautiful golden bubble.

- It is soft and gentle and, as you continue to breathe in and out, you can feel your body relaxing.
- You feel like you are cocooned in a fluffy doona, keeping you safe.
- And very gently the golden bubble lifts off and you are floating.
- Feeling safe and relaxed, you just want to stay there.
- As the bubble floats a little higher, you are being carried over the top of a beautiful garden, and as the bubble reaches the ground you find yourself standing in front of a large wooden door.
- Pushing the door open, you find yourself in the most beautiful room.
- It is your room; the room in the centre of your heart.
- It may appear a bit dusty, a bit neglected, but it feels warm and it's yours.
- I want you to sit in the chair near the window looking into the room.
- See what you have in the room, what you still love, and what you might want to add. Or change.
- If you haven't been taking care of yourself, the room may require a bit of tender loving care.
- Imagine it the way you would like it to be; visualise it, feel it.
- Sit in this room with all the love and support that you need for as long as you want.
- When you are ready to leave the room in your heart, make your way to the door.

- ✻ Move through and close the door behind you, step back into your golden bubble, and float gently back to the place you began.
- ✻ Sit for a moment before opening your eyes and then, when you're ready, open them and return back into your awareness.
- ✻ If you want to, write your experience down in your journal.
- ✻ You can go back to your room any time you want.

Visualization meditation (Guided meditation)

This is a guided visual experience led by a meditation teacher, and involves creating a virtual reality scene within the imagination. This may be something like peacefully swimming with dolphins, or walking in a beautiful garden or forest. It is a good place to start when you're initially trying to quieten your mind.

There are many places to get CDs that have this type of meditation, or you can download them from the Internet. This one can be downloaded from my webpage. Twenty minutes of this form of meditation will help you to feel centred and more relaxed.

Remember the do's and don'ts of meditation from earlier in this chapter.

Read through this part first

Let your brain have its way for a minute. This is often easier said than done, as your brain suddenly realises someone is trying to control it. It takes a bit of practice but keep at it, as it is so beneficial. If it helps, you can find an object to focus on – such as a candle – then begin to bring your thoughts to the task at hand, and concentrate on your breathing. Remember to breathe in and breathe out until you feel you are ready to move into your meditation.

Another way of keeping focused is to find a mental object to train your attention on, whether it is a tree in your meditation forest, a flower in your meditation garden, or you can imagine a candle; whatever works for you.

Forest meditation

- Close your eyes and ask for protection (creating a sacred space). Take a big deep breath; hold it to the count of six then release it slowly. Repeat this up to six times.

- Breathe in through your mouth and out through your nose, allowing your body to relax.

- Now imagine you are on a path leading through a forest. It can be any sort of forest that you like because, remember, it is your forest. It is a beautiful warm autumn day, the leaves on the trees are starting to change colour and you can hear them crunch under your feet as you walk on them. You stop and take a deep breath, breathing in all the smells of the forest.

- You become aware of the trees and how beautiful they are, how majestic they are as they tower above you. Walk towards one of the trees, put your arms around the trunk, feeling the texture and the bark, experiencing the wonderful energy that comes from all living things in nature. Step back from the tree and notice all the other plants that live in your forest. You are aware of the animals but they don't seem to be afraid of you; you feel that you are becoming a part of your forest.

- Sit down with your back to a tree if you wish, close your eyes, breathe in all the smells, allow yourself to relax, feeling peaceful and calm. Open your eyes and observe all life in your forest, feeling relaxed as you do. In no rush – when you are ready – stand up slowly and, as you do, you can see a beautiful lily pond on the other side of a bridge. Make your way towards the bridge and cross over.

- Standing on the bank, you admire the different colours and seem to be drawn to one in particular. Go and sit on the bank near the water lily that you are drawn to. Imagine that you are breathing in the colour; it fills you with peace and contentment. When it is time to leave the lily pond, you realise that you are wearing a scarf of the same colour and it brings you the same feeling of peace and contentment.

* Walking slowly back over the bridge and along the path, you feel different – floaty and really relaxed. When you reach the edge of your forest at the same point where you entered, slowly come back into your awareness; back into the room. When you are ready, open your eyes.

Slowly open your eyes and sit quietly for a few moments, to allow yourself to become present in your mind and body. When we are doing any form of relaxation or meditation, we go into an altered state of awareness so sitting for a moment allows us to come back into our conscious, waking state.

This meditation can be found on the mp3 download on my webpage judithtehuia.com

Meditation for sleep

Prepare yourself as you would for meditation, and create your sacred space.

Visualisation Meditation

* Close your eyes and ask for protection. Take a big deep breath; hold it to the count of six, release it slowly. Repeat this up to six times.

* Breathe in through your mouth and out through your nose, allowing your body to relax.

* Imagine you are in a large four poster bed.

* The sheets are warm and comfortable, and you sink into the bed and feel safe and sleepy. You pull the blankets up under your chin and you are cocooned in a bubble. Just allow your body to relax in this space. Being aware of your breathing, allowing your muscles and mind to relax, you feel yourself becoming more relaxed and ready for sleep.

* Gently come out of your meditative state and you will be ready to drift off.

This will allow you to be in a relaxed enough state to fall asleep.

If it doesn't work the first time, keep doing it, and in time it will work.

Another technique which can be used to help bring on sleep is a mantra – a sacred utterance, or a divine sound, syllable, or word, which is said or sung.

Sleep and kids

There are many reasons why children have difficulty sleeping. It can be that they are staying up too late, that they have bad dreams and are afraid to go to sleep, or they may be hyperactive. They can also pick up on parents' stress.

Helping them to wind down at night and getting them into a good routine is important, just as you do for yourself when you are sleeping well.

Meditation is a great way to get youngsters into a more relaxed state to go to sleep.

In my book *Achievable Enlightenment,* there is a chapter on children and helping them to sleep.

Meditation for kids

Creating a Sacred Space for Children

This meditation is on my webpage.

Children need a sacred space just as much as, or more than, adults do. They don't have the ability to know that they are picking up on other people's energy, or why. Their protection can be their sacred space – a space where their energies are protected from others.

A sacred space for children could be in the middle of a golden bubble where they go when they go to bed, when they are resting, or when they are going to do their meditation. Ask them to imagine what they would want their sacred space to be like. It needs to be quiet and relaxing, where they can sit or lie comfortably.

- ✹ Ask them to close their eyes and imagine the sacred space
- ✹ While they are doing that, you can ask for the best of the best and the highest of the high to be with them as this creates their sacred space.

Exercise: Dolphin Meditation

- ✹ If you are a parent, you can talk the younger children through this meditation. The older ones can read it themselves. Read the meditation slowly a few times, finding a rhythm that works for you. Pay particular attention to your breathing before you get started, and during the meditation don't forget to breathe as well. Don't feel the need to rush. This meditation is available on my website should you wish to download it.
- ✹ Find somewhere comfortable to lie down or sit. Sometimes it's really good to have a pillow and a blanket so you can lie on the floor or on your bed.
- ✹ Close your eyes and breathe in and out slowly. Imagine you are at the beach—it is a beautiful, warm day and you can't wait to get into the water. This beach is a special beach, it is where the dolphins come to play and you can swim and play with them.
- ✹ You sit down on the dry sand, taking off your shoes and your clothes, as you have your bathers on underneath. You walk on the sand down to the water—it is soft and warm, and you can feel it through your toes.
- ✹ When you reach the water's edge, you stop and look—a small baby dolphin comes up to watch what you are doing and beckons you to come and play. You walk out into the water, it's warm and lovely. The baby dolphin swims right up to you, nudging you on the leg and wanting to play. You laugh. You hold onto its fin and it swims you gently along the beach. It is so much fun, and you don't feel afraid. You play in the water

until it is time to get out. When you do, you walk up the beach to where you left your clothes and your towel.

* You sit down on the warm sand and watch the baby dolphin for a while as it swims out into deeper water. Then it turns and looks back at you and you know it's saying goodbye. You don't feel sad that it's leaving, but joyful. You have had a wonderful, relaxing time. When you are ready, open your eyes and come back into the room.

It is much easier when you have the meditation to follow, so at the end of the book you can find out how to get your free copy of the Golden Rose Meditation CD.

There are a few different meditations here for you to try. The more you practice meditation, even if it is only five minutes to concentrate on your breathing, the more you will notice the changes in how you process and deal with different situations in your life.

Checklist

* Laughter is the best medicine.
* Breathing techniques help to relax our body and calm our mind.
* Mindfulness meditation can be done anywhere.
* Meditation relaxes the body and stills the mind.
* It does not need to be difficult.
* Practice makes perfect
* It brings our thoughts into balance.

Chapter 4 - Self-Esteem & Self-Awareness

"Goals directed at being constructive, supportive, and responsive to others, lead to feelings of connectedness, closeness to others, social support, and trust, as well as reduced feelings of conflict, loneliness, fear, and confusion. Compassionate goals appear to engender a sense of worth and connectedness without the devastating drops that come after feedback suggestive of failure."

Scientific American Mind Magazine

What is Self-Esteem?

I'm not surprised that we are a little confused about what self-esteem really is, and what it means to have good self-esteem and low self-esteem.

Self-esteem levels can be found in the answer to: "How do I feel about myself, warts and all?" But where do you find your worth? In the environment that we live in, some think your worth and your self-esteem is found in how well you are doing at school or work, the clothes you wear, and/or the friends you have.

Somehow, it has become caught up with the material value that we place on things. But it's really about considering our strengths and weaknesses and using that knowledge to navigate through life safely.

It is said that we do not inherit self-esteem; we learn it from our family of origin.

Having low self-esteem is having a negative view of yourself. It is often unfounded, but it is where your feelings and thoughts are at a given time. It can often occur when we are in situations where we don't have skills or experience to deal with matters in a rational and calm manner. This can lead us to taking things personally on an emotional, spiritual, and physical level.

Over-personalising situations leads to feelings of unworthiness, of confusion, becoming upset and emotionally blocked. So we act out with self-destructive behaviour, needing to be in control, and losing a sense of self.

This can be changed. It is not always easy, but it can be done.

When we can learn to face our fears and learn from our experiences with the help of a trained counsellor, therapist, or psychologist, we will then have the tools to change these situations around.

So what can we do to help ourselves?

Challenge our negative thoughts

- Fold a piece of paper in half.
- On one side, list five of your strengths.
- On the other side, list five of your weaknesses.

Oftentimes, it is easier to fill up the "weakness" side, and we have trouble filling up the "strength" side. If you are having trouble listing your strengths, think about what your family, friends, and work colleagues have to say about you. Or you can ask them. I think you will be surprised at what you hear.

Have realistic expectations

- When our expectations are unrealistic, we can really knock our self-esteem down. Set small goals and when you achieve them, reward yourself.
- Think about something that you have achieved and how that made you feel.
- Learn to let go of what others think of you. This can be a hard one, but it is worth working on.
- A great way to keep track of your feelings is to have a journal where you write about situations that you have felt good about,

and what you were not so happy about. Try finding something positive to focus on.

One of the best books I have read was called *What You Think of Me is None of My Business*, by Terry Cole-Whittaker, and it's something I try to live by.

Perfection does not exist, let it go

- When we strive for perfection all the time, we are setting ourselves up to fail. Let it go, be kinder to yourself, and realise that nothing in this world is perfect.

- Perfection is how we perceive things to be. What we think is perfect, others may not. It is all in the eye of the beholder. We need to be able to learn from the mistakes we make in order to grow. Go back to "love myself warts and all". This is a really good affirmation to be saying to yourself every day.

A note on affirmations. Affirmations help keep a positive attitude. Having affirmations to say is a reminder to stay in the positive. They should always be in the present tense. An example could be, 'I have time for myself' not, 'I am going to have time for myself'. There are some brilliant ones you can find online; print them out and keep them where you can see them. Choose a different one each week.

Be willing to try something new

- Learning new things is a great way to learn more about you. Personal development is a good place to start when your self-esteem has taken a battering.

- Be willing to adjust your self-belief. What was important a few years ago may no longer be true.

- Stop comparing yourself to others.

To satisfy the need for belonging, build trust.

To satisfy the need for mastery, recognise talent.

To satisfy the need for independence, promote power.

To satisfy the need for generosity, instil purpose.

Checklist

- We are not born with low self-esteem.
- It is unfounded.
- Set small goals and when you achieve them, reward yourself.
- Perfection is in the eyes of the beholder.
- Stop comparing yourself to others.
- Affirmations keep us focused on the positive.

Chapter 5 - Self-care: A Grounded Approach

- Make time each day for yourself. Exercise, in whatever form that it takes, is important for us on many different levels. It could include Tai Chi, walking, meditation, yoga, swimming, or going to the gym. Exercise helps with the endorphins in our brain which, when released, make us happy and relaxed.

- Make time for your personal development, your interests. Identify your needs. You will find that if you have made time for these, you will be happy and others will benefit from this. When you are happy your decisions become more centred.

- Make time to go on a date with your significant other, or go out on your own.

- Understand that you have a right to your own time and that this is vital to your mental, spiritual, and personal wellness. Don't feel guilty about stating this. It is when you don't acknowledge what you need that you will start to lose yourself.

Practical Spiritual Care

By acknowledging your spiritual essence and learning to incorporate it into your daily life, you will also be enriching the lives of those around you. Remember, it is all part of the grand journey that is life. In order to care for others, you must be able to care for yourself. Take time for the little things in life.

- Find time to meditate each day, even if it is for five minutes.
- Ground yourself in your world.
- Have someone to talk to. Solid support around you is important and we all benefit from it.
- Allow yourself time to go to meditation or development classes to meet up with like-minded souls.
- Give thanks for all that you have in your life. The more you do this, the more you will have to be thankful for. Have daily affirmations.
- Taking care of our mental, emotional, and spiritual welfare is really important.
- Find time for yourself.

Helping self

* I can be myself, not what others expect me to be.
* I can change.
* I respect and accept myself.
* I am unique.

Being self-compassionate

> "Self-compassion steps in precisely where self-esteem lets us down—whenever we fail or feel inadequate. When the fickle fancy of self-esteem deserts us, the all-encompassing embrace of self-compassion is there, patiently waiting."
>
> *Kristen Neff, PhD,*

At some point in our lives, we are going to be dealing with change. How we choose to deal with this change is up to us. It can often have a lot to do with our coping skills, our own emotional and mental make-up. But rather than looking at it in a negative light and asking, "why me?", why not turn it around and ask, "why not?"? What skills can I gain from this experience that I can add to my toolbox?

Don't give up or see it as a weakness if you need help to get through some parts. If you had saved up for years and gone out and bought yourself a Ferrari, would you try to service it yourself? Or would you send it to the experts? Think of yourself as the Ferrari; you are worth the investment of seeing an expert. You will be happier, and your work and life will be in balance. Learning how to relieve stress can actually improve your wellbeing and work/life balance, increase your chances of success, and make you a healthier and more efficient person. Most importantly, asking for help can increase the overall quality of your life.

You know that feeling of *"Wow, I've done it"*, and *"I have really achieved something here"*. That's what your life is all about; working through the struggles and getting there and thinking, "I've *done it* and it *feels* great." Those are the successful feelings you get when you work through your life struggles and come out smiling.

Finding some time to spend on your own personal development can be a good first point of entry to stop beating yourself up. We are pretty good at being hard on ourselves at times, but that is not going to change anything. Learn to be your own best friend. You can be there for others – your work colleagues, friends, family – but what about yourself?

Apply some compassion to yourself. Let go of judging yourself so harshly. This can take some doing, but it can be done. It's about grabbing your thoughts before they head off down that road. Stop them, and start replacing them with something positive. It takes practice, but it does and can work.

Exercise in Mindfulness

- When you feel your thoughts are going somewhere you don't want them to, concentrate on doing your breathing exercises; allow your thoughts to concentrate on your breath. Just imagine a lit candle in front of you and concentrate on the flame.

- When your thoughts start to wander, bring them back to the candle but also be aware of what your thoughts are. An example could be, "I can't even meditate, I'm no good at this, how's it going to help?"

- Be aware of the thoughts, but let them go as you bring your awareness back to the flame. Practising this little exercise will help you become more self- compassionate. The more you practice the more you will notice changes.

Negative thoughts really do need to be challenged. If you find that this is something you can't do on your own, then seek out a professional who can help you. You will find them in your local phone book or online, listed under counsellors, psychotherapists, or psychologists.

People who have healthy self-esteem feel good about themselves and who they are. They are able to value their own worth. They are not perfect, as they have their faults, but their faults don't play a major negative role in their lives.

When working through change, it is worth keeping a journal. Think about the people you have around you. Do you have mostly negative people, or people who are positive and make you feel good about yourself? The latter are the ones that you need to have in your life. These people can help you feel good about your strengths, and focus less on your weaknesses. They are people whose focus is on being positive.

Exercise

* Closing your eyes for a moment, I want you to imagine the people in your life. Place yourself at work; in your mind's eye, imagine yourself talking to your friends or colleagues there. How does it make you feel? Happy, at ease, positive, you feel good about yourself when you are with them, or do they make you feel insecure, unhappy?

* Allow your body to really feel these feelings, and learn to trust them. You will start to know the people you want to have in your life and spend time with, and the ones that you don't.

* Find some positive quotes that you love, then download them onto your phone. Have some pictures or positive affirmations on your fridge and computer – wherever you spend your day – just to give you a boost. A couple of mine are:

Devote yourself to an idea.

Go make it happen.

Struggle on it.

Overcome your fears.

Smile. Don't forget:

This is your dream.

Find things that make you laugh. You know how much better you feel when you have been laughing. Find really good uplifting Facebook pages or YouTube videos to follow. Be kind to yourself. If you find you have slipped back, try not to see this as a failure. Just start again. Eventually you will notice a difference.

Live Beautifully.

Dream Passionately.

Love Completely.

Take baby steps; work on shifting habits that no longer serve you, allowing yourself to move into levels of abundance and happiness.

Checklist

* Being self-compassionate is learning to stop beating yourself up.

* Practicing mindfulness helps stop the self-negative thoughts.

* Meditation brings about calm and balance.

* Take baby steps.

* Just concentrating on your breathing brings about calm.

Chapter 6 - Creating Change

"Your life does not get better by chance, it gets better by change."

Jim Rohn

Clutter Clearing

Clutter clearing is a way of creating new flow in your life. To allow the new to take place, the old needs to be cleared out. This can be a physical process, but emotional issues will surface as this process begins. It can range from too many pairs of shoes at the bottom of the wardrobe, to a full appointment book, to 900 emails in your inbox. They can all block incoming change.

To bring about wanted change, we first need to make room for it, so we need to clear our internal, external, mental, emotional, and physical clutter. This can take as long as it needs to take.

Clutter equates to stagnant energy. In order for energy to flow, clutter needs to be cleared.

Your home should be a relaxing retreat that supports your celebration of life. However, if there is too much "stuff" cluttering it up, you can feel mentally overwhelmed with all the things you need to finish. This can lead to subconsciously blocking the flow of energy around you.

Clutter clearing is one of the ways to completely transform your life. You are shifting the energy of your environment, which in turn is shifting the energy of all aspects of your life.

What is clutter?

Clutter is an accumulation of things that impede the flow of energy in your house. Clutter is sometimes tied to identity. It can make a statement about what you are, and represent aspects of your life.

Clutter is any object that you do not love or use, such as:

- Half-finished and never started projects.
- Anything broken or that has parts missing.
- Unwanted gifts.
- Things you might use (but never do).
- Personal letters and old Christmas cards.
- Stacks of old papers and magazines.
- Old make-up (expired).
- Recipes you will never use.
- Expired medication.
- Clothes that don't fit.
- Worn-out shoes.

Remember: Use it, love it, or get rid of it

Common reasons clutter is collected

- It represents security.
- Out of habit.
- It's an inherited pattern of behaviour.
- Fear of lack in the future.
- Evidence of past achievements.
- Unfulfilled dreams.
- Sentimental reasons.

✽ Self-esteem.

✽ Fear that I will not be respected or liked.

Start small. Begin with one drawer, one cupboard, or one small room. Decide how much time you are going to spend de-cluttering. Set the timer, and begin sorting.

There are some things you need to keep in mind as you begin. Ask yourself about each item:

Does this make my energy go up, down, or stay neutral?

✽ Why am I keeping it?

✽ Do I really need it?

✽ Does this really fit who I am?

Then, put it in one of three "piles":

✽ Keep, Relocate, File

✽ Discard, Donate, and Give Away

✽ Unsure

Repeat as needed until your home is clutter-free.

If you are finding it hard to sort your clutter out, ask someone to come and help.

Mental Clutter

Mental clutter: the negative thinking, long-held patterns, the negative chatter that keeps you from maintaining clear thoughts that will empower your life.

Look carefully at the areas of your life that take up a lot of time yet bring you little pleasure. Can you get someone to help and do these tasks for you (housework, ironing, and so on)?

Consider letting go of the areas that demand your time and energy and leave you feeling drained. First, take time to examine your schedule.

✽ Do you have time for yourself?

✽ Have you allowed time for fun, relaxation, friends, and family?

Look and see where your time is being spent. Do this honestly. There is a saying, "Where your attention goes, energy flows."

* Allow time for self-nurturing.
* Make time in your day for creativity, relaxation, and enjoyment. Your soul needs fun.

If there is no time for these things, make an empowering choice today to eliminate non-essentials from your life.

Mental clutter can be over-filling your day – talking, worrying, stressing over little things, or a host of other "got to do" coping mechanisms. By occupying all your time with doing, you never have to face the real issues that stand in the way of the change you want to bring about.

Clearing out the mental clutter – eliminating negative mind-chatter and limiting beliefs – creates room for you to develop an abundant, happy, healthy mindset. Our mindset is reflected in everything we do, think and say.

How do you want to live your life? The choice is up to you.

Begin to clear anything that might represent mental clutter (such as unnecessary papers, out-dated files, magazines, newspapers, or financial receipts), anything you won't be using again. As you clear clutter, affirm: *"I am opening space within myself (or my computer) for mental clarity and focus."*

Continue to ask yourself: If this represented something about me and my life, what would it be? Use the power of image with your clearing. For example, if you have financial difficulties, you might consider going through old bills and financial papers, affirming: *"I am clearing away blockages, and abundance is flowing to me."*

As you continue clutter clearing, continue to ask yourself: If this represented something about me and my life, what would it be?

When one small thing is cleared, celebrate with enthusiasm. Honour yourself for what you have achieved. Congratulate yourself on every little bit of progress you have made.

The Fear of Change

For some, change can be forced upon them due to the fact they don't want things to change at all; never have, never will. In fact, they loathe change. It may be that they are not really sure what they want to change in their lives, or they are just generally afraid of change as it can be scary. Once again, it is about how we look at things.

Others embrace change, and see it as a way to grow and learn. They take it in their stride and understand this is how we experience our mental, physical, and spiritual challenges.

First off, I want you to take a sheet of paper and write down some of the things that you are happy with in your life.

Next, note some things that you are not happy about.

What could you do to change this?

How could you go about it?

Let's look at some positive ways to deal with change, which over time will make things a lot easier for those of us who don't deal well with change.

- Instead of worrying yourself silly about things, get a piece of paper and draw a line down the middle, making two columns.

- On the right side, write down the things you can do something about and on the left side the things you can't.

- Dot point them, then concentrate on what you can do something about and leave the others.

- Write up a management plan or action plan, if you find this helps. Often just writing it down helps to bring clarity to the situation. You will find this really works. Why waste time and energy on something you can't change?

- Often when we take our energy away from trying to sort things out, they sort by themselves – sometimes in a better way than we expected. Wasting time and energy on them is allowing our life to slip away. So make the most of every day and always give thanks.

My favourite saying:

> *"If you don't like something, change it.*
> *If you can't change it,*
> *Change the way you think about it."*

Mary Engelbreit

Changing our mindset

Changing our thought patterns can change our lives. It can be done in a second, and the difference it makes in how we deal with situations is mind-blowing. Think about the ripple effect that is caused by throwing a stone into a pond; changing our mindset has the same impact. You can choose to look at your situation in a negative light or in a positive one; that is up to you. *You have the power to change.* Just be aware of the outcome either way.

Positive thought

Deciding to change your thoughts, actions, and deeds to positive ones will have a life-changing impact. Your body hormones change, your body will feel less tense, and your muscles will heave a sigh of relief. You will deal with situations that arise in a calmer, happier way. If you feel yourself starting to slip back into negative thinking, think of the **STOP** sign, and just tell yourself: "Stop." Don't allow your thoughts to go there. What is it going to achieve? Nothing. You can't change someone else's behaviour; you can only change yours.

Stepping Out of your Comfort Zone

Be willing to fail. Take risks

Are you ready to change?

If you continue to do what you have always done, is that going to bring about the change you desire? Discovering your authentic self means being willing to step into the unknown, being willing to do things differently.

We have all formed habits without us even being aware of them. Habits are formed when we do things a certain way and find that it works. As we continue to use this process, a habit is formed. We fall into forming patterns of behaviour (habits) for many reasons – to protect us from being hurt or humiliated, failing, or being used.

We make our way in the world as best we can, often making many mistakes along the way, but this is how we learn and grow. However, if fear of making mistakes stops us from trying anything new, then we are probably missing out on life's opportunities.

Often, what might be holding you in a situation that is no longer serving you, is not laziness or fear, but the power of your deeply held belief system. To stay deep in your comfort zone through habit – or worse, because of what might happen – could condone you to a life of regret.

Take baby steps; work on shifting habits that no longer serve you, allowing yourself to move into levels of abundance and happiness.

Striving for more

There is no harm in wanting more, but it is important to understand how this will impact on your daily life, health, and wellbeing. My advice is – don't try and force things to happen. If the door is closed to one avenue of pursuit, then find one that is open or allow it to fall into place. Be fully aware of when it's time to stand still and take stock. If you keep getting knocked back, then ask yourself why. Get some help to look at your blocks.

It may not be the road you should be travelling. Look for the signs; they are everywhere. If there is something you want to go for and complete, as one of my teachers would say, "Go ride the wild donkey."

Purpose, what is it?

We all need to have purpose in our lives. It's what gets us out of bed in the mornings. Here are some ways to incorporate more purpose in your life:

- ✸ Have goals and make lists.
- ✸ A treasure map or Vision Board is a good start.
- ✸ Have a positive routine.

This is what I do to include purpose in my day:

My day starts by doing my meditation. In summer, I get up and go for a walk. When I'm walking, I think about all the people I need to thank in my life. I give thanks for what I have. Then I think about what I want to achieve in this day. When I get home I have my breakfast, then I go into the office to work or see clients. I only look at my emails and Facebook twice a day; well, most of the time. I also have my whiteboard marked with what I need to achieve each day. When I have completed each task, I wipe it off.

Checklist

- In order for energy to flow, clutter needs to be cleared.
- Clutter is any object that you do not love or use, such as old newspapers.
- Ask someone to come and help if you are having trouble clearing clutter.
- Changing our thought patterns can change our lives.
- We do have choice as to how we live our day.
- Understanding our lessons can help us to make the most of our lives; working through situations, even more so.
- Be aware of when it's time to stand still and take stock.
- We all need to have purpose in our lives. It's what gets us out of bed in the mornings.
- It's okay to get help to identify blocks that we may have which stop us from moving forward.

Chapter 7 - Where do we Hold & Feel Change?

Unblocking the wisdom of your body

This is a technique that I use a lot with clients and you can learn to use it yourself.

Eugene Gendlin originally developed the Focusing technique. Essentially, Gendlin was interested in situations where cognitive-verbal therapeutic strategies did not work, or where they may have worked for a while but were now ineffective. Given that one may have put in many hours of working with a client, the question is: What to do next?

He suggested an alternative strategy, which involves:

* Stopping the techniques which have been in use up to this point.

* Changing focus; instead of using mind as the seat of knowing in therapy, the body becomes the source of knowledge and direction.

* Acknowledging that a great deal of our daily life is orientated and directed by body sense, insofar as we make assessments of persons, situations, tasks, etc., many times over and without cognitive reflection. Our actions tend to be guided by "felt sense", which we refer to as intuition or a hunch.

So focusing is a way of dealing with issues by having the body direct us, and it depends upon our being in a *relaxed state*.

There are six steps in focusing. Note that once you start to practise it, you won't need to have your notes handy all the time.

- Clearing a Space

    Take some deep breaths, concentrating on your breathing. In front of you, you can see a space or a room. If you see anything or anyone in the space, I want you to stack it up against the back wall or far side of the space. Now I want you to push the space out further so that it becomes larger. If any thought, feeling, or person comes into the space, just stack it up against the back wall.

    Push the space out even further, so you can hardly see the edges and the space you have is very large. If any thought, feeling or person comes into the space, just stack it up against the back wall. Now push the space out again so you can no longer see the edges at all.

    I now want you to bring a thought, worry or concern back into the space. I would like you to pay attention to an area within your body – the abdomen area. Now see what comes when you ask, "How is my life going? What is the main thing for me right now?" Sense or feel the response within your body. Let the answers come slowly from this sensing. When something comes, do not go inside it. Stand back and say, "Yes, that's there. I can feel that there." Let there be a little space between you and that. Then ask what else you feel. Wait again, and sense. Usually there will be a few things.

- Felt Sense

    From among what came, select one personal problem to focus on. *Do not go inside it. Stand back from it.*

- Name

    What is the quality of this unclear felt sense? Let a word, phrase, or an image come up from the felt sense itself. It might be a quality-word. Like tight, sticky, scary, stuck, heavy, jumpy; or a phrase; or an image. Stay with the quality of the felt sense, until something fits it right.

* Resonate

   Go back and forth between the felt sense and the word (phrase, or image). Check how they resonate with each other. See if there is a little bodily signal that lets you know it is a fit. To do it, you have to have the felt sense again, as well as the word.

   Let the felt sense change, if it does, and also the word or picture, until they feel right in capturing the quality of the felt sense.

* Ask

   Now ask: What is it about this whole problem that makes this quality (which you have just named or pictured)? Make sure the quality is sensed again, freshly and vividly (not just remembering from before). When it is here again, tap it, touch it, be with it, ask it, "What makes the whole problem so..? Or ask, "What is in this sense?"

   If you get a quick response without shift in the felt sense, just let that kind of answer go by. Return your attention to your body and freshly find the felt sense again. Then ask again. Be with the felt sense until something comes along with a shift, a slight "give", or a release.

* Receiving

   Receive whatever comes with a shift in a friendly way. Stay with it a while, even if it is only a slight release. Whatever comes, this is one shift; there will be others and you will probably continue after a little while, but stay here for a few moments.

If, during these instructions, you have spent a little while sensing and touching an unclear holistic body sense of the problem, then you have focused.

It doesn't matter whether the body shift came or not. It comes on its own. We don't control it.

✻ Thanking

Give thanks for what you have received.

Chapter 8 - Sleep, Fatigue and Rest

"Sleeping is no mean art: for its sake one must stay awake all day."

Friedrich Nietzche

What is sleep?

Understanding how the lack of sleep can impact on an already over-burdened body and mind is another tool to add to your toolbox. Knowledge is power.

Every night, most of us undergo a remarkable change. We leave waking consciousness and for hours crisscross a backdrop of dreams and deep sleep.

When we wake, we remember very little about the hours that have just passed. Although everyone sleeps, even for just a few hours, most people would be struggling to define sleep. We rarely contemplate or appreciate that we are sleeping while we are asleep.

Sleep is characterised as a state of changes in psychological functions, such as breathing, heart rate, body temperature, and brainwave activity. During some stages of sleep the brain is just as active as when we are fully awake.

Scientists have noted the following characteristics that accompany, and in many ways define, sleep.

* Sleep is a period of reduced activity.

* Sleep is associated with a typical posture, such as lying down with eyes closed in humans.

- Sleep results in a decreased responsiveness to external stimuli.

- Sleep is a state that is relatively easy to reverse (this distinguishes sleep from other states of reduced consciousness, such as hibernation and coma).

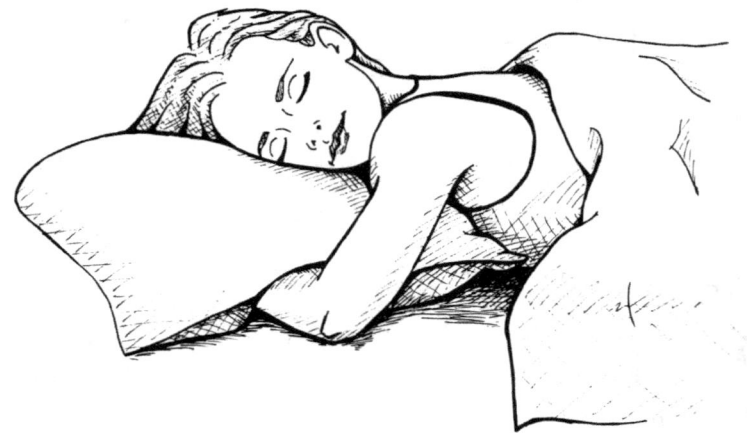

Stages of Sleep

There are two types of sleep – non-REM sleep, which is the really deep sleep that our bodies require, and REM sleep which is when we dream. The best sleep is when we can get into deep REM-sleep.

The National Institute of Health states that the human body carries out a number of crucial tasks during sleep to help maintain good health, so that we can function at our best. Not getting enough sleep can be dangerous for both our physical and mental health, but many people find it hard to fall or stay asleep.

NREM (non-rapid eye movement) sleep is the period when our heart and breathing rates are slow, and blood pressure drops. The person does not move about much.

NREM sleep is divided into three or four stages:

- **Stage 1 sleep** – *the transition period between wakefulness and sleep. There is slow eye movement. Alpha waves make way for Theta waves. If someone in this stage is woken*

The Toolbox

up, they think they have not been asleep. *Hypnic jerks (involuntary twitches) commonly occur during this stage.*

* **Stage 2 sleep** – *50% of our sleeping time is in* Stage 2. The heart and breathing rates slow right down. The eyes do not move at all. People hardly ever dream during this stage. Even though the sleeper is quiet, they can be easily awakened.

* **Stages 3 & 4 sleep** – *used to be divided into 3 and 4, but is now more commonly grouped into just Stage 3. Stage 3 used to be the transition period between 2 and 4, when delta waves started to occur. Delta waves are associated with deep sleep, and dominate Stage 4 sleep. There is some dreaming in this stage, more than in stages 1 and 2, but much less than in REM sleep.*

REM (rapid eye movement) sleep – a normal stage of sleep that makes up between 20% and 25% of total sleep time. There is rapid movement of the eyes and low muscle tone.

* Babies spend much more of a night's sleep in REM than older people.

* Humans generally experience four or five periods of REM sleep during a typical full sleeping session; the last one is longer than the first.

* Some people may have a brief period of light sleep, during which they are easily awakened, shortly after an REM session.

* Sleep experts say our brain neurons are about as active during REM as they are when we are awake. However, atonia paralyses the body during REM. Atonia is an extremely relaxed state of skeletal muscles.

* If we remember a dream, it would have occurred during REM.

To get to these stages, we really need to be physically tired – not over-tired or mentally tired, but tired. Therefore it can be beneficial to go for a walk in the fresh air, for a bike ride, or a swim – whatever you find you enjoy doing. Being forced to do something means we will not enjoy it, and it will end up having the opposite effect from what we were trying to achieve.

Let's have a look at our own sleep patterns. Tick them off, and then write a little about each one. Think about your day – writing down what you do during the day can really help give you a much clearer picture of what you really are doing. Write down the areas where things need to change and what you could do to achieve this.

Questionnaire

Check out which ones apply to you. Place a tick beside them:

1 - I have a job that involves shift work or night work. ☐

2 - I frequently travel across times zones. ☐

3 - I have a new baby, or baby is teething. ☐

4 - I feel that sleep is a waste of time. ☐

5 - I enjoy sleeping very much. ☐

6 - I usually sleep with a bed partner. ☐

7 - I get seven hours sleep a night. ☐

8 - I wake up during the night and can't get back to sleep. ☐

9 - I can't get to sleep because I'm worrying about work. ☐

10 - I wake up feeling tired all the time. ☐

Do's and Don'ts

Don't get caught up in the cycle of needing sleeping pills. They are okay in times of crisis, but only for occasional use. They mess too much with the normal physiology of our sleeping cycles.

Wind down before sleep. Do your meditation, or have a cup of camomile tea. Find your own ritual that works for you.

Lack of sleep can be debilitating, as mothers, shift workers, zone travellers, and students, well know.

Sleep deprivation can lead to learning difficulties, lack of concentration, fatigue, and often-impaired judgement, which in turn can lead to accidents happening.

Sleep is just as important as food and water in order for our bodies to function efficiently. The problem is that a lot of us don't get the amount of sleep our bodies really require.

Cause and Effect

Lack of sleep can be dangerous

Symptoms of Fatigue

Some of the symptoms of lack of sleep and fatigue can include:

- Feeling groggy when waking in the morning.
- The tendency to dose off when not being active.
- Poor concentration and being irritable.
- Constant yawning.

The cause can be many things:

- New babies and young children keeping you up at night.
- Shift work, travel to different time zones.
- Busy lifestyles, illness, colds and flu.
- Some medications.
- The sleeping environment, too hot or too cold.
- Your partner snoring, or it may be poor sleep hygiene; having too much caffeine too close to bedtime will stimulate the nervous system, making sleep less likely.
- Lying in bed worrying about things instead of relaxing and going to sleep. Eventually lack of sleep takes its toll.
- Stress can have your brain wired, so sleep seems impossible.
- Living too close to a motorway or train tracks, or both.

The normal amount of sleep required for an adult

Most adults require around seven to eight hours of sleep per night, so what happens if they only get six? This two-hour loss of sleep can have a major impact on how they function during their day. It can cause:

- A slower than normal reaction time.
- Reduced awareness.
- Impaired judgement.
- Lack of concentration.
- Irritability and moodiness.
- Poorer memory.
- Decreased motivation.

It certainly isn't the best time to be driving heavy machinery.

Signs you're getting enough good sleep

- You fall asleep within 20 minutes of lying down.
- You don't usually wake up more than twice a night (which you may not even remember).
- You don't feel tired during the day.
- You're able to focus on what you're doing.
- You have enough energy throughout the day.
- You're not irritable or moody.

Well done for having the sleep your body requires. You have probably been in that place where you have been short of sleep and know what it's like, so you have worked out a routine that works for you. Keep it up, and again well done.

Getting good sleep

Here is a list of tips and tools. See which ones work for you:

* Waking at the same time every day, and going to bed at the same time each night. Setting a routine really helps.

* Try not to have alcohol, cigarettes, and caffeine before bed, as they can make it harder to get to sleep and cause your sleep to be unsettled.

* Try reducing TV or computer time in the evenings. Take TVs out of your bedroom.

* Try not to nap during the day, as this will make it harder to sleep in the evening. In saying that, if your body requires a nana nap then have a short one; 10 minutes can make all the difference.

* Exercise first thing in the morning, or on your lunch break. Getting outdoors in fresh air can do wonders. Raise a slight sweat when doing it. By exercising, we release tension. Sunlight can help reset your body clock.

* Learn relaxation and meditation techniques to help you switch your mind off in the evenings.

I know there are those who require less sleep, but busy women really need seven to eight hours. These tips have been tried and tested, but not all of them will work for everyone. If you're really struggling, the best and easiest way to work out how to get sleep is by working with a doctor, counsellor, psychologist, or sleep specialist.

Exercising near bedtime tends to raise your heart rate and can interfere with sleep, so morning or lunchtime is the way to go. If you catch the bus or train to work or home, get off a few stops earlier and walk. This allows you to exercise, get fresh air, and can also be a good time to think and be in a better space by the time you get home.

Sleep and Meditation

In an earlier chapter we talked about how meditation can help in many areas of our lives, and meditating before going to sleep has many benefits. When you are ready to go to bed, getting yourself into a healthy routine is good.

If you are physically tired, meditating before sleep will put you in a good space to drift off into the deep REM sleep that is required for the healthy healing of our bodies.

There are many relaxation meditations available. Try out the ones that I have in the meditation chapter.

Questionnaire

Look at these questions and work out just how much time you are spending on outside activities that could be reduced in order for you to get more rest.

1 - How many hours after school are dedicated to kids' sport/training/hobbies?

2 - How many hours after work do you spend at the gym/hobby?

3 - How many hours are spent with the kids on the weekend at sport?

4 - How many hours a week do you spend on chores?

5 - How many hours do you work?

6 - How many hours a week do you travel for work?

7 - How much time do you spend on holiday actually resting?

8 - Do you feel rested after a holiday?

9 - Do you find Xmas or Easter relaxing?

10 - Do you have any people in your life who are obligations rather than pleasure?

11 - Do you have people in your life that you find draining?

12 - Do you spend your free time watching TV?

13 - How many hours a week do you actually rest?

The Toolbox

Sometimes our lives get so out of control that we have not realised just how exhausted we have become, until something major happens to stop it. This can also be used to look at your children's lives. Do they need to be doing all these activities? Or could the time be used to allow them to rest and have a much more balanced lifestyle?

Checklist

* We now have an understanding of the importance of sleep.
* What sleep is.
* What we can do in order to improve our sleep pattern.
* Setting up our sacred space.
* Balancing our lives to have more rest.
* Where we can go to get help.
* What happens when we are suffering from lack of sleep.
* Relaxation meditation for adults and children for sleep.

Chapter 9 - Nutrition for the Time-Impaired

"Time is a created thing. To say 'I don't have time' is like saying, 'I don't want to'."

Lao Tzu

Why eat well?

You have heard it before: Eating well is really good for you. The reason you have heard it is because it is true.

Denise Linn, in her book *The Mystic Cookbook,* said, "Food is so much more than food, your approach to it can open up pathways to spiritual renewal."

Whenever you are preparing food, or about to eat it, treat the food with the respect it deserves. Make this time a joyful time, not just a chore. Give thanks for it and eat with the intention that the food will heal and strengthen your body.

Sharing, learning, and cooking a meal is quite a spiritually healthy thing to do, as it replenishes the soul and is so good for the digestion.

We need food to fuel our body, but it is what we eat that makes the difference.

When you eat a well-balanced diet:

* You will have a lot more energy.
* You will feel good and look healthier.
* Your immune system will function as it should.

- Your thoughts will be clear and you will find that you handle stress better.
- The likelihood of you getting diabetes, cancer, and cardiovascular disease, will decrease.
- There are so many things that can influence our eating habits.
- Our emotions.
- Our mental wellness.
- Being time-poor.
- A lack of funds.
- Being too tired to cook.
- Physical illness.

Whatever the reason, there are ways to change this. It doesn't have to happen straight away, it can be gradual. But having a *healthy attitude* will certainly go a long way to changing things. In the short term, poor eating habits can contribute to many health issues such as stress, tiredness, and our ability to work.

Changing eating habits

Having the right attitude goes a long way if you seriously want to change your eating habits. Work on changing your attitude and giving thanks. Use positive affirmations. Ask for help when you need it.

Here are a few tips that can help:

- Take baby steps, just trying one thing at a time. Making too many changes at once can lead to disaster. Or to no change at all.
- Start with something easy – introduce a piece of fruit or a salad, or both if you want, on the first day. Just work your way gradually into what you want to achieve.
- If you struggle with three meals a day, break them up into six smaller meals.

* Experiment with various foods and see which you like.
* Try not to skip meals.
* Don't cut everything out completely, just decrease the amount. You are more likely to stick with eating well if you allow yourself to eat less healthy foods once in a while.
* If you don't like a lot of veggies, juice them. This is healthy and you are still getting your required amount of healthy food.

Food that we should be eating

We need to eat plant foods regularly. These are fruits, vegetables, grains, seeds, and nuts. Eat a little red meat if you want to – it is high in vitamin B12 and that is good for you.

Whether or not to eat red meat

In her article *The Real Beef About Red Meat*, Nancy Clark, M.S., R.D. wrote,

"Fifty-plus years ago, most athletes were meat-eaters who believed that beef was the best foundation for a sports diet. Steak at dinner converted into bigger biceps by breakfast. Red meat instilled toughness and aggressiveness. But today's athletes have changed their tune:

'I'm repulsed by the idea of eating an animal.'
'I want to eat less fat and cholesterol.'
'I'd rather eat more carbs to fuel my muscles.'
'I want to avoid the hormones added to meats.'
'Meat is fattening.'
'I don't like the taste.'
'I don't cook meat. It leaves a mess to clean up.'
'I don't like to kill animals.'

Whether or not you choose to include red meat in your diet is up to you. However, it does provide an excellent source of high quality protein.

Red meat provides iron and zinc, two important minerals for optimal health. Given this, confusion abounds regarding the pros and cons of eating beef, pork, and lamb. Perhaps you have wondered if you or your family should eat or avoid red meat.

The answer is not a simple yes or no but rather a weighing of nutrition facts, ethical concerns, personal values, and dedication to making appropriate food choices. Yes, you can get the nutrients needed to support you from vegetarian food sources... but are you?

Growing at Home

Growing your own veggies can be fun, especially if you encourage your children to help. It has been proven that when children help grow veggies, they are more likely to eat them, which will benefit everyone in the long run. I know you might think, "But I don't have time for this." It doesn't need to take long, though, and you will find that being with plants is a way of relaxing. You don't have to have a lot of space; they can be grown in pots and taken with you if you rent. It's relaxing and healthy – you know what you are eating because you have grown it.

The longest time spent is the actual planting; decide if you want to grow from seed or seedlings, which have already been started for you. Decide what you want to grow.

Always ask your friendly nurseryman or woman what you need to do to look after your plants, as it depends on where you live and the climate. It is so much fun going out each day to see that a seed you planted the week before has popped through the soil and in no time will be providing you with your own food source.

You will need to spend a little time in looking after the plants, so let's look at growing them in pots if you don't have time – or space – for a garden.

Most plants can be grown in pots. And the actual pots don't need to be expensive. Shop around; we get ours from our local tip. Give them a good wash when you bring them home. They need to be placed in a sunny spot, but in summer when it's hot they will need some shade.

You will need some good potting mix, and you will need to water the pots at least twice a week, maybe more in summer. Feed them with dynamic lifter or a seaweed-based liquid fertiliser every four to five weeks in their growing stage. But the effort is worth it.

Try herbs, tomatoes, spinach, lettuce, broccoli, and cucumbers. In fact, give anything a go and if you are not sure, ask your nursery person for help.

Top Australian author and medic Dr John Tickell says that the greatest rule of nutrition is the two-thirds and one-third rule, so here it is.

If you eat two-thirds of plant food and one-third of refined or flesh food, you are doing well. Just keep on doing it.

Potential Health Impacts of Poor Nutrition

Case Studies

1 - Shift worker

> Peta is a shift worker. She gets up at 2.30am to be at work by 4am.
>
> She has nothing to eat before leaving home, as she doesn't have time. At 8am she will have either toast and marmalade, or porridge, or cereal, with a cup of coffee.
>
> 10am could be more toast, or fruit, or chocolate, or biscuits.
>
> Home time is midday or 1pm, and she will have KFC sometimes, or fish 'n' chips, or noodles from the noodle shops, or leftovers from last night's dinner.
>
> At dinnertime as a family they have rice, chicken, veggies, or red meat and veggies, or takeaway, or seafood. In two years she has put on 20 kilos.
>
> Peta has just been diagnosed with type 2 diabetes and is now on a weight loss program, so her eating habits have changed dramatically. She is also working with a dietician to work out a meal plan which caters for her work hours. She doesn't want to stay at her job but says, "For now I need to." Before going to work she now has a piece of toast and a cup of tea and, with the help of the dietician, the diabetic educator, she feels that she is getting back some control over her life.

2 - Busy Working Mother

> Jenny is a busy mother of four children, ranging in the ages of five down to eighteen months. Her day begins at 5am. Her

husband has already been up for an hour and has been to the gym. Together they get the children ready for their day at crèche, but she doesn't have time for breakfast. She is out the door and the children are dropped off at crèche at 6am. She catches the 6:30am train to work, which takes an hour.

Her breakfast consists of a coffee when she gets to work. Her days are busy and there is not much time for her. At morning tea, she will have biscuits and a coffee. During the day she will consume at least one or two small cans of Coke. For lunch she usually buys food from the hospital canteen, or takes leftovers from last night's dinner. She admits she does not drink enough water throughout the day. She is home by 5:30pm. Her husband cooks tea and that will consist of fish, or meat, salad, or veggies. She only eats tea if she is really hungry.

Jenny is a classic example of a busy working mother with no time for herself. She isn't sure what she can do to change it. But with some thought, planning, and a real will to change, her day could be improved.

The impact of poor nutrition on our health

According to the World Health Organization, an unhealthy diet is one of the major risk factors for a range of chronic diseases, including cardiovascular diseases, cancer, diabetes, and other conditions linked to obesity. Specific recommendations for a healthy diet include: eating more fruit, vegetables, legumes, nuts and grains; cutting down on salt, sugar and fats. It is also advisable to choose unsaturated fats instead of saturated fats, and working towards the elimination of trans-fatty acids. Improving dietary habits is not just an individual problem, it is a social one. Therefore it demands a population-based, multi-disciplinary, and culturally relevant approach.

Risk Factors

- Type 2 Diabetes
- Stroke
- Some cancers
- Gout
- High cholesterol/Heart disease
- Hypertension
- Obesity
- Tooth decay
- Osteoporosis
- Depression
- Eating disorders

Eating healthy

Eating Plans

These days it can be hard to feed yourself, let alone a whole family. Here are some tips to feed everyone and save some money.

- Think about bargain shopping, getting together with other mums and bulk buying.
- Scour the junk mail if you get it, or look at it online.
- Aldi have good cheaper products.
- Try and plan your weekly meals. This allows for a weekly shop and as you know what you're having for each day, there is then less stress.
- On Sunday nights, or morning if you're working nights, spend some time working out the menu.
- Place the menu on the fridge so you and the others in your house know what you're having.

The Toolbox

- Delegate some of the jobs. Peeling potatoes, etc.
- Prepare ahead if you can. I know that there will be times when you are just too tired, but planning is the key to being able to enjoy some healthy meals.
- Make lunch to take to work. It costs less and can be a lot healthier.

Enjoying your meals

- First thing in the morning, have a glass of warm water with some lemon juice in it. Make sure you sit down for your meals and eat with your family, not at the bench or on the go. It's also about honouring your food and allowing your body to digest it. This allows for your body to slow down and relax.
- Have a think about your meal times – is there anything you could do to change them in order to create a relaxed atmosphere where there is time to enjoy your food?

❋ Don't skip breakfast

It is the most important meal of the day. I know it's easy to tell yourself it's not important to eat breakfast, but it is. You are breaking your fast. Your body needs energy at this time of the day to help it function well.

You are less inclined to eat unhealthy foods if you have had a good breakfast. Take it to work if you haven't got time to eat it at home.

- ❋ Another good tip is to have smoothies – ones you can make yourself. Anything goes here.
- ❋ Take some snacks, fruit, and nuts, cut up veggies with some hummus dip. Whatever you like.
- ❋ Another tip is to make the lunches the night before. That gives you a bit more time in the morning to sit down and enjoy your breakfast.

Good nutrition and regular exercise are essential for a healthy mind and body.

Good sleep patterns are important for being able to have a productive day. It's all about nurturing and taking care of yourself.

Checklist

- ❋ Don't skip breakfast.
- ❋ A little thought and planning can go a long way.
- ❋ Changing your attitude to food can make all the difference.
- ❋ The impacts of poor nutrition.
- ❋ Growing your own veggies and herbs.
- ❋ Why we should eat healthily.
- ❋ Treating food with some reverence and giving thanks.

Chapter 10 - Dreams and Nightmares

*"They've promised that dreams can become true
But forgot to mention that nightmares are dreams too."*

Oscar Wilde

Carl Jung believed that dreams were a way of communicating and familiarising yourself with the unconscious. Dreams do not conceal your true feelings from the waking mind, but are a window to your unconscious. They serve to guide the waking self to achieve wholeness, and offer a solution to a problem you are facing in your awakened state.

I have found that when I don't stop and listen to my gut feelings or the signs around me during the day, I end up having a very real dream, one where I'm left wondering if it was real; the kind where you can get up, get a drink of water, then go back to sleep and it just carries on right where it left off. For me, it's a way for my subconscious to say, "Hey, just stop for a moment, I'm trying to help you here." It can often be making meaning out of our lives. If we have experienced some sort of trauma, or major loss, repeated dreaming about the events or situation feels more like a nightmare but often it can be trying to tell us something. You may have dreamt that someone was trying to tell you something or give you a message, but because they may have died you don't want to go there and you don't want to listen. But it could also be your subconscious trying to attract your attention.

Our minds and bodies are amazing because they hold the key to our healing if we let them. But when we feel that everything is out of control and nothing is real, we don't want to trust so the vicious cycle of being out of control continues. There are alternative ways to receive healing, but if you decide this is the path you want to follow – perhaps you feel you have nothing to lose as nothing else has worked – first check out whether or not the person has the skills and ability to help. One of the things that worked for me was dreamwork.

Dreamwork

Dreamwork is a way of uncovering messages from the unconscious mind. It is a very powerful tool in helping us think outside the box. Dreamwork offers unique opportunities for exploration of dreams, oneself, one's problems, and one's potential all at once, in a safe and supportive setting.

About five years ago I was unable to work. I was suffering from post-traumatic stress disorder due to being bullied and intimidated at work in an acute mental health facility. What made things worse was that the return to work officer kept harassing my doctor and me.

I didn't think I would ever feel confident to go back to work; I felt powerless, and not in control. A friend encouraged me to go and do a Transpersonal Counselling course with her, which was the best thing I ever did as I was able to become familiar with Dreamwork. Through that life-changing experience, I now have the tools to help myself if that memory ever reoccurs.

I have enclosed my session to help you understand how it works.

Dreamwork Sheet

Name: Judith Te Huia
Date: 16/04/2010

Description of dream:

Yew, my Guide, said, "Come follow me." We walked until we reached a hill and then we stopped. He said, "I want you to look at the hill." It was a gentle hill with long grass and trees, the scene was very pretty. He said, "Look at it again, but this time with your third eye." It was different; there was a stone wall around the hill with a large gate that was locked with two I Ching coins, interwoven. Yew said, "I want you to unlock them." I was thinking, "And how am I supposed to do that?" When I concentrated on them with my third eye, not my normal vision, I saw that they were opening and we walked through.

Feelings:

My time with Yew is precious as I learn so much. I was thinking, "I wonder what we are going to do today." I was excited, in anticipation, feeling that I knew so little, but the day was beautiful and I love the countryside, so was happy to be there. When he asked me to look at the hill in front of me, that was something I could do. Then he asked me to look with my third eye. I could do that as well, so I was feeling okay about that. But when he asked me to unlock the I Ching, I thought, "You have got to be kidding." There were butterflies in my tummy, but I went into my meditative state and focused with my third eye and couldn't believe the gates were opening. I thought, "How did I do that?"

Metaphors suggested by the imagery:

David and Goliath

Personal information relating to emotions of the dream to recent events, thoughts and feelings

The feeling of not having the ability to do what was asked of me was paramount. Not having the faith or belief in myself, I struggled with the simplest things. The feeling of being powerless was overwhelming. I was not in control of anything.

Waking context:

I was unable to work, due to suffering from post-traumatic stress disorder, having been bullied and intimidated at work in an acute mental health facility. But it didn't end there. I was then being bullied by the return to work officer who just kept harassing my doctor and myself.

Pre-dream thoughts:

Am I ever going to get out of this situation? Am I going to be well enough? Will this get better?

Associations, integrating metaphors and waking context:

The feelings of "I can't do this". I was feeling very small and insignificant, but in my dream I overcame the problem by believing I could.

Realising I can do this, I can move on, I can have control over my life and, no matter my size, I can win.

Active Imagination

> I: Why have you brought me here?
>
> Y: To get you out of your environment.
>
> I: I do like it here.
>
> Y: I needed to have you where you feel safe.
>
> I: Okay.
>
> I: Why are you asking me to do this?
>
> Y: So that you can recognize that it is safe.
>
> I: It is beautiful. The hill is peaceful and beautiful.
>
> I: I don't think I can do the next part.
>
> Y: Just try, you are not looking beyond the present moment.
>
> I: But I can't.
>
> Y: Yes you can, and when you do you will see your potential.
>
> I: I did it. It looks very different.
>
> Y: Yes, this is how you can learn to move forward by using the other parts of your awareness.
>
> I: Oh.
>
> Y: Now I want you to unlock that awareness.
>
> I: I don't know how to do that.
>
> Y: Do what you did before and just focus.
>
> I: Okay. I did it. I don't know how I did it but I did, wow! I unlocked that complicated looking lock, and I can move forward now.
>
> Y: Can you see by shifting your focus you have been able to move from the pain you were in, and you are able to walk through the gate to the future, and let that part go?

I: But if I didn't have you I would still be stuck.

Y: You would have moved forward, as you can move through the different states of consciousness with ease.

I: Thank you, I will see you again.

With a lot of the tools that are in this book, along with Dreamwork and Cognitive Behavioural Therapy, I got well and was able to move on with my life.

Dreamwork is one of the tools that I have in my work practice, along with Past Life Regression, Crossing Over, Counselling, Meditation Classes, Transition Coaching, and my Clarity Sessions. If you feel I could help, please get in touch with me.

Gratitude Journal

Over the years, researchers have found that writing things down can help us to organise our thoughts. In essence, it helps us to see the meaning of events going on around us and to create meaning in our life.

Robert Emmons, a University of California professor, is one of the world's leading experts on the science of gratitude. Here he shares his research-based top tips for keeping a gratitude journal.

- Don't just go through the motions. Research by psychologist Sonja Lyubomirsky and others suggests that journaling is more effective if you first make the conscious decision to become happier and more grateful. "Motivation to become happier plays a role in the efficacy of journaling," says Emmons.

- Go for depth over breadth. Elaborating in detail about a particular thing for which you're grateful carries more benefits than a superficial list of many things.

- Get personal. Focusing on people to whom you are grateful has more of an impact than focusing on things for which you are grateful.

* **Try subtraction, not just addition**. One effective way of stimulating gratitude is to reflect on what your life would be like without certain blessings, rather than just tallying up all those good things.

* **Savour surprises.** Try to record events that were unexpected or surprising, as these tend to elicit stronger levels of gratitude.

* **Don't overdo it.** Writing occasionally (once or twice per week) is more beneficial than daily journaling. In fact, one study by Lyubomirsky and her colleagues found that people who wrote in their gratitude journals once a week for six weeks reported boosts in happiness afterward; people who wrote three times per week didn't. "We adapt to positive events quickly, especially if we constantly focus on them," says Emmons. "It seems counterintuitive, but it is how the mind works."

Once again, with this practice don't rush it. Work out what best suits you. Like the Focusing techniques, you need time to allow yourself to get the most out of them. But for me they work. Keeping a gratitude journal keeps things in perspective.

The Toolbox

Checklist

- Dreams can be a tool to help us heal.
- For me it was my subconscious saying, 'Hey, we can help you deal with this?'
- Dreamwork is a way of uncovering messages from the unconscious mind when we are ready to address them.
- Change does not have to be fearful.
- We can learn to embrace it and step out of our comfort zone.
- It is okay to want more, but not at the expense of our health.
- Letting go of past conditioning can really help us move forward in a positive way.

Chapter 11 - Treasure Maps & Vision Boards

Do all things with kindness.

Treasure maps and vision boards are an ideal way of bringing everything together, helping you focus on the areas in your life that you would like to work on and change.

It is a time to reflect on all the tools that you have in your toolbox and the others you would like to gain in the future. It is a time to celebrate your life and where you are heading.

Treasure maps and vision boards can help us focus on the changes we want to make in our lives, by having a vision of how we see ourselves in a year or two years. It could be how we would like a project we are about to embark on to look; the difference having a holiday would make in our lives. It is a way of setting goals that are achievable, and some that are way out there. The main thing, though, is that it is fun to do – and it works.

In times past, ceremonies, rites of passage, and rituals were performed as a way of connecting to unseen realms. These ancient rituals allowed people to tap into the answers held within.

In today's modern age, we still use a variety of tools to gain insight. Creating a treasure map or vision board can be used as a ritual or ceremony to reach this inner knowledge. It opens us up to receiving the messages from our higher consciousness and guides, allowing them to assist us on our path towards spiritual awareness, abundance, and everything else that we are striving for.

It's a really fun thing to do, and a chance to put on paper some of the things you would like to achieve or change in your life. Before you begin, here is a list of things you will need:

The Toolbox

- Piece of coloured cardboard (a colour that you love, and as large as you want).
- Magazines (to cut out pictures).
- Scissors.
- Glue.
- Pencils.
- Glitter.

Here are just some suggestions that you may want to use for your treasure map or vision board, or you can just use your imagination – anything's possible.

Sit down and think about some of the long and short-term goals that you may have. Some of the things you desire may seem out of reach, but remember it is your treasure map, so whatever you think you want, put it on the lists. When you have never done this before it can be hard to work out what is important and what isn't. But as you're thinking about it, write it down and then go over what you have on your list. It takes time and a bit of thought to really know what you want to achieve in life. What you may have wanted to achieve when you were twenty will most likely have taken a back seat to what you may want at thirty, forty, and so on. With time and maturity, things change and what may have been important once can lose its intensity.

Meditation for your Treasure Map or Vision Board

Before you start on your treasure map, it's worth doing a short meditation for some inspiration.

- Read the meditation to yourself a few times, slowly, finding a rhythm that works for you. Pay particular attention to your breathing before you get started, and during the meditation don't forget to breathe as well. Don't feel the need to rush. Have your journal on hand to write down your thoughts and feelings afterward.

* Create your Sacred Space. Close your eyes and ask for protection, breathe deeply and hold it to the count of six. Release it slowly. Repeat this up to six times. Breathe in through your mouth and out through your nose slowly. Set your intention of what you hope to achieve from this exercise.

* When you feel you are starting to relax, imagine you are walking in a field of wildflowers – all the colours you can imagine. As you walk through the field, smell the perfume of the flowers, breathing in their beauty. When you find a clearing near a stream, sit or lie down near a tree and feel the long, soft green grass beneath you. Be aware of the tree you are resting near. Watch as the leaves move gently with the breeze, and the light as it streams through the leaves. Think about what you want in your life as you relax.

* Stay in your field of flowers for as long as you need, and when you are ready to come back, walk back through the field of wildflowers, bringing with you a sense of peace and beauty. When you have reached the point where you arrived, gently open your eyes and come back into the room.

Think about what you wanted when you were in meditation and write down your thoughts, dreams, and wishes in your journal. Decide if they are going to be on your treasure map. You can set it out in any fashion you like, perhaps like a road map, or have it as a flower with each of the petals as another goal. You can be as creative as you like; just let your imagination run wild. For instance, you may want to lose weight. All you need to do is imagine your goal weight, the clothes you will wear, and the food you will eat. On your treasure map or vision board, you can display the pictures you have found in magazines or on the Internet of the new you.

You can always get a few friends to come and do it with you; it really can be a lot of fun! Interestingly enough, you just may find that your friends also have goals they have never discussed. It can encourage a much deeper friendship and understanding between you on a more

The Toolbox

personal level than you thought previously, and an understanding that everyone has dreams and hopes deep within.

Make sure that some of your goals are practical and achievable, not for instance, "I would like to fly to the moon." One day, of course, it might be possible for every man, woman and child, especially with the way things are going with technology. But it's just a matter of making sure that you don't get disheartened if your goals take a while to happen. The rest can be as wild and whacky as you want, just keep practicality in mind.

Put your treasure map somewhere you can see it. There is not much point spending time making one only to put it away and never see it again.

When you achieve one of your goals, put a star beside it, tell someone, and reward yourself because you deserve it. Your treasure map is, in a sense, a very large affirmation; a physical representation that anything is possible. These maps are brilliant at helping you get through difficult times, and offer great promise for the future.

Sometimes you will find long-term goals can be achieved quite quickly, and the ironic thing is that some of the short-term goals can take longer. The main thing is that it instils hope that any of your dreams are possible and realistic. When it comes time for the goal you have set to come to fruition, ticking it off will give you a sense of accomplishment and a potent realisation that your goals are very achievable.

When you have attained everything you wanted, it is time to redo the treasure map and think of new inspiring aspirations you would like to accomplish. Follow the same process and remember, each time you achieve a goal, reward yourself.

What is your passion?

Think of when you were little. Most of us were going to grow up and be something or someone. Some of you will have been really passionate about certain things. I was going to be a farmer, nurse, or vet. But farming for me was what I really wanted to do. Somehow it wasn't where my life ended up, but I am still passion about conservation, the environment, and I love gardening. I did become a nurse, then a counsellor – still with the caring and helping profession, just more about people rather than the planet.

Don't let fear stop you

Fear is one of the most debilitating things that anyone can go through. It is such a waste of energy and it can stop us in our tracks. Often it is more about the fear itself than the actual situation fear is around. One of the most wonderful tools to use when working with people suffering from fear is a technique I learned in Transpersonal Counselling. It is called 'Focusing', and was devised by a man called Eugene Gendlin – and it works. You read about it a few chapters ago.

So I am going to say here: Do not let fear stop you from achieving your dream, ambition, or goal. There is help out there to get you through it.

Checklist

* Treasure maps and vision boards are ideal tools for change.
* We can create them for any situation in life.
* A new job, home, next stage of your journey, holiday or adventure.
* We need to learn to step out of our comfort zone.

Farewell for now

Dear Robin,

When I wrote to you at the beginning of this book we were about to embark on a journey together. Over the months I have watched you grow; become more willing to ask for help. You have added tools to your toolbox, made big changes in your life and are quietly confident about your future. Yes there were times when you struggled and wanted to give up, but you dusted yourself off and had another go.

I will walk by your side for as long as you need me, but one day soon I will watch that beautiful butterfly spread its wings and fly.

Love

Judith x

There is a lot of information in this book. I hope you will be able to take something from the information and the meditations, and expand on the tools you already have in your own toolbox.

Take time to work through the exercises, as there are quite a few. The more time you spend on them, the more you will notice the benefits. Don't be hard on yourself; you may find that one week you are doing really well and the next week not so well. That's okay, it's life. Just don't give up, as in the end it will be worth it. It was for me.

Life was never meant to be all work; it's about creating that ideal work/life balance and bringing fun and happiness back into your life.

I have a Meditation CD called the *Golden Rose Meditations*. For those of you who buy this book, you will receive one free. In order for this to happen you will need to contact me on my website judithtehuia.com and tell me the page number that the Relaxation Meditation is on, along with your name and address. If you would rather download them, then the same thing applies, but you will be sent to another page where this can happen.

References

Aron, E. N. (2003). *The Highly Sensitive Child*. London: Thorsons, Harper Collins Publishers.

Barker, P. (2003). *Psychiatric and Mental Health Nursing: The Craft of Caring*. London: Arnold, Hodder Headline Group.

Beyond Blue: www.beyondblue.org.au, worldwide web 2015.

Elder, R., Evans, K., Nizette, D. (2005). *Psychiatric and Mental Health Nursing*. Elsevier Australia.

Gendlin, Eugene T. (2003) *Focusing*. London: Rider, Random House.

Kruse, E., Chancellor, J., Ruberton, P. M., & Lyubomirsky, S. (2014). **An upward spiral between gratitude and humility**. *Social Psychological and Personality Science, 5,* 805-814.

Linn, D., Linn, M. (2012) *The Mystic Cookbook*. Hay House America.

How do I locate help?

Australia
For After Hours crisis counselling, or traumatic incidents.
1300 361 008

Beyond Blue: www.beyondblue.org.au or info line: 1300 22

Crisis Line: 136 1694636

Directline: (Drug and Alcohol) Counselling 800 88 236

Lifeline: 13 11 14

Men's Line: 1300 789 978 (24 hour Counselling)

Judith Te Huia: Counsellor and Holistic Therapist judithtehuia.com. Phone: +61 422 142 729

Resources

The Way of the Peaceful Warrior, Dan Millman

There is Always Help; There is Always Hope, Eve A Wood. M.D

Embracing Change, Tony Buzan

Learned Optimism, Dr Martin Seligman

You Can Do It, Paul Hana

The Art of Happiness, Dalai Lama and Howard C. Culter

Emotional Intelligence, Daniel Goleman

The Road Less Travelled, M. Scott Peck, M.D

Golden Rose Meditation CD, Judith Te Huia, www.judithtehuia.com

3 week online Meditation Course, Judith Te Huia, www.judithtehuia.com

Biography – Judith Te Huia

For 30 years Judith has been running an intuitive practice, which has included meditation classes, creating and facilitating personal and spiritual development courses, running seminars, participating in festivals, as well as seeing individual clients for counselling, intuitive readings, and past life regression. She also helped her husband to teach Tai Chi classes, and worked with the intellectually disabled for several years.

In early 2000 she became a carer for her husband when he developed a life-threatening illness, which is now controlled. This spurred her to go to university at the age of 55 and gain a degree in nursing, and then a diploma in Transpersonal Counselling. Judith has worked predominantly in mental health since 2000 and has seen, first-hand, the terrible damage which stress, anxiety, and depression cause to good, hard-working people.

Her motivation for writing about grounded living practises comes from seeing people getting tied up in the world of not feeling worthy enough, working all the hours that God gave them to blot out how they are feeling, and then suffering terribly as a consequence.

Judith is planning a series of retreats over the coming year, and runs live and online courses in self-development.

She lives in Sunbury, Victoria, with her husband, Hully.

www.ingramcontent.com/pod-product-compliance
Lightning Source LLC
Chambersburg PA
CBHW070543300426
44113CB00011B/1772